Remembrance: The Second Generation

EVELYN FREILICH

Copyright © 2018 Evelyn Freilich

All rights reserved.

ISBN: 9781728765853

DEDICATION

To all who were impacted by the Holocaust.

CONTENTS

   Acknowledgments   1

1 Joyce Hess   5

2 Carol Barnett   7

3 Susi Erwin   12

4 Marsha Pinson   14

5 Joan Greenbaum   21

6 Sam Devinki   24

ACKNOWLEDGMENTS

Thank you to all who contributed to this book. I know that writing a personal letter to your parents or recounting stories about their horrifying experiences was not an easy thing to do. I sincerely hope that your stories impact others as much as they did me.

I also want to thank Sonia Warshawski for inspiring me to undertake this project. After she came to speak at my school, I immediately began thinking of ways to ensure that survivors' stories are always remembered. As the Holocaust is only briefly taught in the classroom, it is extremely important for people of my age to read about first and second generation personal stories in order to truly understand the effects of the Holocaust. Therefore, I hope the following stories are able to provide people with new perspectives about the Holocaust and encourage them to keep remembering and learning about it.

JOYCE HESS

Dear Mom,

It's been 11 years since we last spoke. Your passing left an indelible scar on my heart. There are so many times I have wanted to call you and share life events, both good and bad. You would be so proud of how we continue to carry on your legacy. I served as President of The Midwest Center for Holocaust Education and have continued speaking to schools, just like you did. Now I know how you felt after each speech that you made to students. The love and engagement these students exhibit is amazing. Their vision of the world is impacted by your story. It has been my commitment and passion to continue to tell your story so that the next generation can choose love over hate.

Your son carries on your legacy of commitment to a shul by serving as President of his synagogue. You taught us that you can create a live long community through your synagogue.

Your grandchildren carry your soul in their hearts. They continue to practice your Jewish traditions and commitment to community. Kate is a teacher, serves on the Council of Advocates for MCHE and is expecting her first child in October! Alex opened her own dance studio and loves it! It's so fun to hear them use the Yiddish terms you taught them in their everyday lives.

As I've grown older, raised my own children and now anticipating the birth of my first grandchild, I can reflect on how much I admire your strength, intelligence and perseverance. Based on how hard you struggled to survive and the pain and heartache you went through, it has given me a different perspective on you and the life you lead after the war. You have provided me with the ability to face adversity with a positive approach. You have provided me with the soul to give back to my community. You have provided me with the Jewish upbringing and traditions to give me an inner peace. You have provided me with the knowledge that family and friends are everything and we should cherish each moment with them.

Thank you for providing us a future without burdening us with your past. It must have been so difficult to hold on to those memories for a lifetime. You showed us that it is possible to start a new life no matter what the past may hold. I just want you to know that the impact you made on our lives will live on to future generations. You are always in our hearts!

Your loving daughter,

Joyce

CAROL BARNETT

Dear Mom and Dad,

There isn't a day that goes by that I don't think of the two of you—all the lessons you taught us, the opportunities you gave us, and the love you showed us. What makes me appreciate/admire/marvel at you even more so is knowing so much and, in some respects, so little, from where you came.

Dad—you rarely, *if ever*, talked about your past. Here's what I know…you and your parents migrated from Düsseldorf to Stillwater in 1937 (you were 13), essentially with just the "shirts on your backs". I can't imagine the sacrifices/choices you had to make. Your fears. The family/friendships you had to leave. I don't even know how many family members you lost at the hands of the Nazis. Recently, I learned you were one of the "Ritchie Boys". Amazing.

Mom—not sure where even to begin. You were a total rock star. When you would meet others, if they detected your accent, they may have asked you, "Where are you from? You have a lovely accent." Without missing a beat, you would boldly reply, "San Francisco." If that response didn't pass muster, they'd look at you skeptically, and then may follow up with, "Where were you born?" You'd reply, with definite finality in your voice, "Europe." That was the end of THAT.

I remember when I was growing up, occasionally, I would ask you a question about your parents. After all, most of my friends had three or four grandparents still living. We had one (Dad's mom (Dad's dad died in 1958)). You'd answer vaguely that they had died a long time ago, then quickly changed the subject. I didn't give your response much thought…until one summer when your aunt (we called her Bibi) visited from San Francisco. Though I don't recall exactly how the topic came up at dinner one night while she was visiting, it was then that I first learned that you were a Holocaust survivor and your parents were killed in the camps. I can't remember what I said, if anything at all. I was too stunned/scared.

For many years after that fateful evening, a part of me wanted to ask you questions; another part of me was terrified to do so. I remember once, somehow we started talking about your past and I asked, "What was it like to be on the train?" You simply replied, "Which time?" Wow...

As time went on, you'd share snippets of your story with some of us in the family. You didn't want to talk about your experiences during WWII; it was too painful. You didn't want others to have pity for you. In fact, you'd probably be pretty ticked I'm even doing *this*.

Finally, at the beginning of 2014, you agreed to share your whole story with me. Maybe because you thought I could finally handle it...I'm really not sure why, but I was so grateful you did. Sadly, I only captured one interview. It was in the spring of 2014 and you passed away very unexpectedly seven months later. I've listened to bits of the interview a couple of times since you passed away, not to hear the content, but to hear your voice. You probably think that's silly. I would sacrifice almost everything to have another interview with you...

Mom, you were one of the bravest people I will ever know. Of all the stories you shared, by far, the most compelling one was that of your last days with your mom. You and she were at Teresienstadt. It was the end of October 1944. She was on a list to go to Auschwitz, but you weren't. A guard told you not to go. You didn't care. You went anyway. In fact, you jumped to get on the train to be with her. When you arrived, she was told to go left and you to the right. She went to the gas chamber and, of course, was exterminated. It was the last day the gas chambers operated there. I remember when you shared that story, I asked you how you could possibly go on. You said you made up your mind that day to "go forward". "Forward" became your mantra for the rest of your life. There you were, 18, no mother, no father (at that point, you didn't know where your brother was, if he even was alive), truly, starved to a skeleton-like silhouette, and with no promise of a tomorrow. But, you defied all odds. Not only did you survive; you thrived.

You always reflected that you had three lives: your carefree childhood in pre-war Germany, the Hell existence of the Concentration Camps, and your fulfilling adulthood in the United States. You and Dad met in San Francisco in 1947 and married in 1949. You lived your life "Forward". Mom of four, you worked part time in Dad's family business on/off forever, until Walter and I were in high school, when you went back full time, pretty much until you passed away. Dinner was at 6:30 p.m. sharp. Homework was finished before dinner. Breakfast was at 7:15 a.m. sharp. Beds were made before breakfast. You even set the breakfast table the night before. You did that forever, too. You were the consummate hostess and an outstanding chef. Dad always bragged your home was the best restaurant in town. To this day, *no one* can make Nestle's Toll House Cookies as delicious as yours. You loved loved loved the arts—both visual and performing. I remember going to art galleries with you and we'd always find the Impressionists' rooms first. Then, we'd each pick which work we would take home if we could wave a magic wand to do so. You had an amazing musical ear (even though you "would turn milk sour" when you sang, as do I, which you reminded me of constantly). You knew composers, names of their works, and could even cite the key.

You loved to travel. One of my favorite trips with you was when we went to Italy the summer of 2014 and you climbed to the top of the Leaning Tower of Pisa in the pouring rain. The guard was in disbelief of your age. When we went to Israel and Jordan in 2004, you rode a camel. You strode across the High Line in NYC a couple of years later.

You took hot yoga until you were 80; you weren't very happy with Loren (cardiologist) when he recommended you just do regular yoga. The Rose Garden at Loose Park was your sanctuary. I was just there a month ago for the first time since you died and had a good cry. It was purging. God, I miss you...

When I came home from the hospital after Samantha was born, you began to request I call you every day to check in—at first, I thought your request was ridiculous. It became a routine for us...always. Sometimes the conversation was as short as this, "Hi, Mom. How was your day today?" "Fine. Busy. I went to yoga, then the office for awhile, then to the grocery store. And, I just finished dinner." "Great. Talk to you tomorrow. Good night, Mom." I can't tell you how many times I've wanted to call you at the end of the day. It might be about a recipe question. Or a story about the grandchildren. Or about lunch with Rosanne. Or Samantha's latest sale she made at the gallery. I can't erase your contact info off of my phone or out of my address spreadsheet. I finally tossed out a worn-out pair of shoes of yours the other day.

So, Mom and Dad, here's why I've agreed to write this letter. Sadly, and worrisome, the "second generation's" awareness of the Holocaust is frighteningly and pathetically low. Anti-semitism in the US is clearly on the rise. Dad, how I wish you were here to discuss politics. You were so incredibly smart and a voracious reader. You loved sharing articles and cartoons with us. Doing so was one of your hobbies.

According to claimscon.org: (an organization whose mission statement includes, "Going forward we must ensure that future generations learn the lessons of the Holocaust to preserve the memory of those who suffered so much and those who were lost."). *There were over 400,000 camps and ghettos during the Holocaust. 49% of Millennials cannot name a single one.* Rosanne led the Shoah program this spring at the Jewish Community Center and shared Al's story; then, another friend, Joyce Hess, shared her mom's story at the Johnson County Library. This summer, I watched the movie "The Big Sonia". After those three events, I decided it was time to share your stories. This fall, I'm hoping to go back on MCHE's Second Generation Speakers' Bureau. While you may disagree and disapprove, I can't sit silent. Your story shaped us. I hope I can do the same for our children, grandchildren and beyond.

I love you and miss you both.

SUSI ERWIN

Dear Mom and Dad,

As we approach this Rosh Hashanah it is with bittersweet reflection. We ALWAYS celebrated before services with a big dinner first then schlepped downtown to Bartel Hall. I remember quite vividly, going shopping with you mom for a few new "Temple" clothes. The 6 of us looked rather dashing by 1950's standards. For today our look would be quite dorky. As tradition would have it, Dad you ALWAYS brought wrapped candy to keep us awake, the problem was the noise of the unwrapping. Funny that 2 days ago, Former President Bush handed Michelle Obama what appeared to be an unwrapped piece of candy. Dad I think you would have laughed out loud. But even more poignantly, before Bush and Obama spoke in honor of John McCain, Henry Kissinger spoke. Oh how you loved Kissinger!! You looked like him, sounded like him and in my eyes you were just as brilliant as he, though I could have sworn he was already up there messing around with you!! Just how old is Kissinger anyway? I think you are 97.

I remember at times being embarrassed that my parents and grandparents had such thick accents. I remember the quirkiness in my contemporary home. No one ever understood the Frank family. We were so different. Mom cooked koenigsberger klopse, galactus, tongue, wienerschnitzel and other delicacies too weird to mention. Dad played the harmonica and tuba and sang in a barbershop quartet. Looking back I can't help but believe most friends and acquaintances thought us to be strange, yet quite funny.

Today is so different. I'm still by myself after 17 years. Mom, I know you ALWAYS worried about me. But I'm ok! I have the best and biggest family to call my own. Kim, with her husband Todd and 3 kids, Max and Ben who were Bar Mitzvahed in the last 4 years and sweet Eli who will have her Bat Mitzvah next week, on her actual 13th birthday Sept. 8th the day before eve of Rosh Hashanah! Boy, would you both be thrilled to be part of this celebration! I'm excited beyond belief and incredible proud of Eli. Danny has been a successful ER Doc in Durango for the last 12 years and his family is amazing. Todd has taken over Ron's business, has a most beautiful wife and family, living not too far from me in Denver. I'm guessing you have Sandy under your wings just like Kenny. I miss them as well so very much, especially this week while packing for Eli's Bat Mitzvah in LA.

Thank goodness Syl will be there with her significant other Eric, whom I adore, and LEX. Syl is doing well. We lean on each other more than you know.

I guess I have totally missed the point of this letter, but truthfully, because we never heard stories from that terrible time in both your lives, I could not reflect on what it means to be the child of a holocaust survivor other than bits of what I have now shared. Mainly we were just a quirky big family growing up in the only place we knew, KC.

So I will say goodbye for now. Just know I dream, imagine, wish and hope you all could be physically present...until that day, I cherish all the memories and pray you are ALL good. Dad, I know you are singing with the angels!! You have a magnificent voice I still hear today!

Love you so very much,

ALWAYS, Susi

MARSHA PINSON

Dear Mom and Dad,

I write to you at the request of a young girl who is afraid that her peers are not learning the truths about World War II and the Holocaust. Carol Isenberg Barnett has asked that some of the children of the survivors of that time help her to understand more so that she can share the truth, as we know it.

I felt lucky to be reared by you and the remnants that we called "The Family" or "The Crowd." These were the courageous friends who had witnessed and suffered the worst that humanity can produce and yet NEVER gave up on life, hope, and love. You taught your children those values and that you, who came to America with nothing, would provide us with the best education that we could achieve. You dealt with the past in different ways and viewed Germany in opposite ones. Mother, you always said you could go back to see the country of your early years—the beauty, the culture, the Land of Schiller and Goethe. Dad, your anger became hatred of all things German, including automobiles and electronics. And still, to meet a cousin once again, you agreed to go to Dusseldorf to meet her on your last trip to Germany—finding forgiveness, at last.

I know much more of your story, Mother, from your birth in 1920 until your privileged world came to an end with Hitler's rise to power in 1933. Your family, proverbial big fish in the little pond of Dinslaken, were respected members of their town and of their Jewish

Community. Your father traded in skins as his business and served on the Board of the distinguished orphanage that put your small town on the Jewish map: the Weisenhaus (the Orphanage). From an early age, you were at home there and you refused to wear a tunic and rucksack that would be better than the children who lived there. Your mother, like her 3 sisters in neighboring towns, owned a couture hat and accessory store. The women would share their sales and needs with one another by phone each night and they would travel together to Paris for fashion shows to keep au courant with their wares. You lived a privileged life with maids and a chauffeur, but your wise mother still insisted that you learned the basic tasks of a household telling you, "If I knew you would grow up to be a princess, you would not have to learn to make your bed." This wisdom and your strong sense of what was fair and right saved your life and theirs, in the end. You had a darling brother, 4 years your junior, and summers were spent at the shore of Nordernei, with other friends and nannies; Jewish holidays and traditions were celebrated, and life was filled with friends, Gentile and Jewish. When you were no longer allowed to go to school in your little town, you switched to a bigger school in Duisburg, the next bigger town, where you were the star pupil. You had dreams of becoming a doctor. When you were also dismissed from the second school, you had your mother arrange for an English tutor, whom you met at a dear friend's home in Duisburg. By this time, your best friend would cross the street to avoid interacting with you, as her father had joined The Nazi Party and she was in the Hitler Youth Organization.

With your mother's help and over the objections of your father, you sought a visa to come to America. Your father's cousin would not agree to bring over a girl of 16 or 17 years but a close friend turned to her relative, Herman Stern, of Valley City, ND, for help for you. She vouched that you could cook and take care of a home and knew that you would never be a burden to anyone. Uncle Herman, as we grew to call him, trusted his relative and brought you over in March of 1938, as he did 123 others. You went alone to Stuttgart to get your papers and packed your trunk under the watchful eye of a Nazi soldier. Your mother had gotten you the best clothes that she could, including a fur coat but the rules of emigration were strictly obeyed. When you said goodbye to your father at Hamburg, you felt you might not see him again but you always thought you would see your brother again. You left behind an elegant home filled with art, silver, culture and the memories of a family filled with cousins and beautiful celebrations of anniversaries, birthdays, and even your brother's modest Bar Mitzvah, in 1937. Your favorite teacher refused to say goodbye to you…and you knew it was time to go. Your skeptical father learned that you were right in the worst way on Kristallnacht, when agitators from another town came into your home, ransacked and destroyed what they could, and arrested him. After his release, he arranged to leave Dinslaken for the much larger city of Essen with your mother, and to send your brother, Erwin, to a farm in Holland on a Kindertransport to be safe. You had an aunt and her Dutch husband with their 3 children who lived in Amsterdam, so that seemed a good plan. They left their home one month on December 10, a month after the Pogrom. They lost all that they had worked for and enjoyed. On Kristallnacht, the children of The Weisenhaus, including 2 of your cousins, were marched through the town dragging a wagon—many to perish in the years to come. You had a letter from your brother about those terrible days but it was he whom you never saw again.

You arrived in New York City, knew your cousin, who informed you that you had a place to stay for a few days but that you had to find a job the next day. You changed your name from Tea Eichengruen to Dorothy Eichengruen, on the advice of your cousin's husband, also a refugee, who said your name needed to sound more American. By now, you had lost your home, your homeland, your education, and your financial support, and even your name. You lived on less than fifty cents a day and saved enough to get tickets for your family to leave Germany, only to have them lost. You pledged that you would repay more than $750 to bring your parents and brother to America in summer of 1941, not knowing how you would ever have that much money. Luckily, your parents did make it out of Lisbon somehow on the last boat with Jews in September of 1941. Tragically, your brother's visa and tickets were lost in Amsterdam. He was deported to Westerbork in February, 1942, with one of his cousins, thinking that they would leave the others alone. Uncle Erwin died on his first day at Auschwitz on September 29, 1942. You and your parents would learn of the deportation in a cryptic telegram and confirm the truth many years later. Now, his name is memorialized in the Anne Frank House in Amsterdam and a sculpture of the rough cart that dragged the children stands in Dinslaken to remember the lost Jews and a smaller piece stands before your home commemorating your mother's shop. We attended the dedication to the former together as the few remaining Jews of Dinslaken gathered with 2000 residents of Dinslaken. The Ecumenical Council and the City Council arranged for our return for a week of reunion when the monument was unveiled so that the horror experienced during the Holocaust would never be forgotten. There was redemption in our visit and a renewal of your old friendship with your best friend.

To this day, I have a relationship with some of our hosts.

Ironically, Dad, if you had been alive, we would never have made the trip back to Dinslaken. You thought trips like ours were half-hearted attempts to expiate collective guilt. Had you met the people we encountered and heard their intentions, you would have been amazed at the Germans' facing history so as NOT to repeat it. I knew much less of your story after Hitler came to power, Dad, other than the sad fact that you were kicked out of Medical School in Cologne and returned to Duisburg, your hometown, to work in your father's store. Your mother had died in 1929, when you were 16, and your father, not an easy man, was bereft. His sister, he was one of 8, who was just 10 years older than you, came to help take care of the household. You became very close and were able to return her love 10 years later, when you gave Manya and her husband the affidavits they needed to come to America. I also learned by accident really, that you were in Hamburg waiting to leave, when your father took his life. Your sister had a civil marriage while you were still in Duisburg; but the Jewish ceremony was a few days later when you had gone. Your father did not have a way to get out of Germany, you were gone and your sister was getting ready to leave with her husband, who had passage to New York. The stress of being left behind was too much. You did not learn this news until you arrived in America. Your visa came from your mother's cousin and took you to Kansas City, where you started life again as an orphan.

The people who were gathered thanks to Cousin Oscar, became our family and included many to whom we were not really related at all. You stayed in touch with the woman who would become your wife and in August of 1942, visited her in Seattle, where she had moved with her parents, and the two of you decided to marry. October 11, 1942, with you in the Army at Ft. Leavenworth, was your wedding day. Mother received permission to travel to Kansas City from Seattle, because Germans were "enemy aliens" and subject to curfew and restricted travel because they were living on the West Coast after Pearl Harbor.

Dad, I am so sorry to say that I have now learned much more about the terrible times you endured in Germany from 1933 to 1938, from a document that you wrote for your Commanding Officer titled "GERMANY between 1919 and 1941: FROM DEMOCRACY TO NAZI-ISM." In 93 pages you give your understanding and explanation of how Hitler could possibly have come to power in the advanced country of Germany; how he studied the psychology and history of the German People and set his plan in print in *Mein Kampf*, only to be misjudged, indulged, and feared by most of the world until it was too late. I think of this as your thesis—amazingly well-written, after your 3.5 years in the US. It is here that I learned some of what you saw and experienced such as: "I went to school in Germany from 1919 until 1933 and I have seen how my teachers were sabotaging the new democratic government…Hitler recognized this situation and his chance to get hold of this German youth." "According to Hitler's theory the Jews were responsible for everything and they were to be blamed for everything…from the beginning, nothing was done by Hitler without giving a reason..And if you constantly keep on telling lies, finally people believe these lies. ..Free press was abandoned…And Hitler realized that he would have to find another way of eliminating his opponents, or as he called them 'enemies of the state.'" Opponents were arrested and killed or never seen again or cremated and their remains sent to their families—with a charge for the shipping! Fear was rampant. Spies were everywhere. Putting many dissatisfied Germans into uniforms and giving them guns and power over the police created an environment of cowardice and terror. You knew of a man who worked in the Krupp Factory making munitions, which were illegal after the Versailles Treaty. He told his wife, who told a friend and soon, he left for work one day and never returned. "One other case about the activities of the Gestapo is fresh in memory" when 4 Union officials were working before Unions were outlawed and beaten to death at their work and then buried in a forest. When found, the Official explanation was that they committed suicide! Your beloved Latin teacher refused to begin each day with "Heil Hitler," and twice asked to be discharged, but he was needed and forced to go against his principles. He died a year later in an insane asylum. In Summer of 1933, you were going into the Courthouse when another Jewish citizen was walking out. A Nazi in uniform was patrolling the street, drew his pistol, and shot the man to death, saying that the man "had laughed about me and I did not like that." He was never even tried.

You describe Hitler's campaign against everything that would remind the people of previous times that involved burning Communistic, socialistic and all literature written by Jews to be burned. It was an awful view to see these Nazi-hordes gathered in public places to celebrate the killing of the spirit of the past democratic epoch by this gesture of burning the proof of modern civilization." At the time, Jewish students and teachers were banned from schools and universities, you were in Medical School, and even though a small percentage of students could stay, they had "to wear yellow armulets if they wanted to continue their studies…but I quit as I would not continue under such dishonorable conditions. " You "intended to continue your studies in France or Italy, but this was also made impossible when the government refused permits to take out money out of Germany." Although you had left, you describe the beating of your uncle in his small town in November, 1938,, where your family had lived for 100s of years. He was sent to a concentration camp and his non-Jewish neighbor, who tried to stand up for him was arrested and tried as a traitor. You sum things up saying, [the boycott of Jewish businesses] "That was the start of a life which became more horrible from day to day. Storm troopers would do as they pleased since they were the masters…the mob of unemployed bandits became the highest authority. I have lived though this time and I have seen that honest, square people did not dare to go outdoors as they had reasons enough to be afraid somebody might beat them to death without reason…or for the reason that they had been faithful to their own ideas."

I am sorry that you kept your sadness to yourself, Dad, but so very grateful for the values and love that you and mother did share with Joan and me. Your spirits are with me and my children every day.

JOAN GREENBAUM

Dear Mom and Dad,

A young woman whom I don't know has asked me to participate in her project: What would children of Holocaust survivors and refugees tell their parents about what they learned from them?

The first thing that comes to me like the 11th Commandment is Survive, Live. Also, from that commandment, I learned to understand that it is a duty not to take life lightly and to take care of it (sometimes a little too protectively). Appreciate it fully, the good and the not- good. That doesn't mean love every minute of it, for it is not all lovable. But know that life itself is important. Make it count. Mom, as you in particular would say, just by surviving we win. We keep those who want to exterminate us from achieving their goal, and we show we are more powerful than their hate. Be strong in the face of hate.

You both, and Grandma and Grandpa, had terrible experiences and losses great and small. With your actions and your words, you all taught me to go forward, one step at a time, one day at a time. Do what is necessary to do, even if it is hard and even if not everyone agrees. And when you get to the bridge you have to cross, cross it as best you can. It is possible, indeed imperative, to make a life, though it is different from the one you thought you would have, but one that has joy and love and laughter.

Does it seem obvious to say that from you I have my strong sense of being Jewish? Of course it does. You were persecuted for your religion. Part of the importance of being Jewish for me is the duty to honor you and your commitment to being Jewish. We would discuss (occasionally argue) about Judaism. Is it a religion, a peoplehood, a culture, a tradition? All of the above, some of the above? You were fierce in your Judaism, however you defined it. For me, it is a given, as integral to who I am as being female.

You taught respect toward people of other races, backgrounds and religions. Probably you would have had those values, anyway; but I feel that you insisted on them because you and your families and communities had been subjected to bigotry. You knew first-hand what happens when prejudice and intolerance lead to hate. I learned from you to resist expressions of prejudice, to stand against them. You encouraged and supported my involvement in social justice actions and groups from the time I was a child.

Three principles I have from you that I think—I hope—guide me. "Do justly, love mercy, and walk humbly with your god", the definition of god not being important. "Don't judge another until you have walked in his shoes". "I know that I know nothing". The second, Dad, didn't extend to the "German character" We would actually argue about it. I would say you can't hold succeeding generations accountable for what their parents had done. You said the German character was the German character and that the next generations were the same as the older ones. It was an instance of your demonstrating respect for another person's ideas, even though, as I later recognized, mine may have been hurtful. The third was the injunction to keep learning, keep an open mind, not to believe everything you think you know. All three are grounded in a commitment to be better than the perpetrators of the Holocaust and the people who abetted them.

Finally--for this letter-- you gave me family, our family and the sense of the absolutely critical importance of family. I am blessed beyond words and measure for the foundation of love, support, and connection I have from you and our immediate and extended families. Your home and a large part of your family community were taken from you. You made a new one. I know that I, and my family, will always have the connection to that family. I have a sense of being grounded because of the ties to that family. Strangely, I don't have a feeling of having a family history that goes past my great-grandparents (though intellectually I know that is not correct and that there are family trees to prove it). You gave me a sense of rootedness in a group bound by strong ties. That feeling may not be unique in situations like ours, but it is exceptional and special. I am grateful for it every day.

Love always

SAM DEVINKI

Part 1:

Wodzislaw to WWII

Revised 12-2-11

It was beshert that in Wodzislaw, Poland, somewhere around the turn of the 20th century, Moshe Dziewiencki would meet and marry Kaileh Jachimowiecz, and Shlomo Braun would meet and marry Rivka Rosenberg. "Beshert" being Yiddish for, "meant to happen by God."

The town of Wodzislaw, "Voyjislav" in Yiddish, is situated in swietokrzyskie province, on the Mozgawa river, (the right tributary of the Mierzawa river), atop the hills of Garb Wodzislawski. More specifically, on the road from Miechow to Jedrzejow, it's about 8 miles SSW of Jedrzejow and about 34 miles NNE of Krakow.

By merging three small Slavic settlements, the Polish Prince Wladyslaw Opolski founded the town and funded a monastery there in 1257. The proud emblem of Wodzislaw today is the left facing profile of a fire breathing lion, with a line through the "L" in Wodzislaw like some people put a line through the number 7.

It was a farming community at its founding, but in the 13th and 14th centuries, heads of the Polish state urged the Jewish community to create a business community and gave them enough self-rule to do so. This was a much better deal than Jews received in most of the rest of western Europe. It even served to shelter Jews from the Christain Crusades in the 14th and 15th centuries. Allowed to prosper, they did. Artisans, merchants, and service providers thrived there. Somewhat ironically, about mid-way through the 16th century, Wodzislaw was recognized as Poland's center of "Calvinism;" the beliefs and doctrines of the Protestant Reformation generally credited to Frenchman, John Calvin.

By the 17th and 18th centuries Wodzislaw was a hub of Polish Jewish affairs. Many highly regarded rabbis came to serve in Wodzislaw; from Menachem ben Zalman Gabais, to Shmuel ben Uri Shraga Phoebus, to Eleazar Loew, (1758-1837), a Jewish legal authority who was born there.

Each Jewish community, or Kahilla, was led by a governing body, or Kahal. A Kahal was like a municipal government and dealt with the day-to-day concerns of the main town, and whose authority extended to the surrounding villages. These local governments were run by elected officials. There was also a system of regional councils with representatives from all over Poland that were associated with the national governing body, the "Council of the Four Lands."

Annexed by the Austro-Hungarian empire in 1795, Wodzislaw became part of the Grand Duchy of Warsaw in 1809, and then part of the Russian Empire in 1815 - which dubbed it the "Congress Kingdom of Poland." Fifty-five years later, in 1890, Jews lost significant civic rights as a result of Russian control, but by that time some 1,500 Jews called Wodzislaw home. Among them were Rivka Rosenberg, Shlomo Braun, Kaileh Jachimowiecz and Moshe

Dziewiencki.

At the turn of this century, the year 2000, Sam Devinki, Solomon Moses "Sam" Devinki, the great-grandson of Moshe and Kaileh Dziewiencki, commissioned genealogies from Phillip A. Applebaum of Applebaum Research tracing the family history and heritage back four generations,, encompassing six separate families. From them we know that the name Devinki was originally Dziewiencki and that it comes from the village of Dziewi"czyce in the district of Pinczow, Poland.

We also know that the Devinki family name should really be spelled Dziewi"cki, not Dziewi"czyce, nor Dziewiencki, much less Devinki as we know it today, but the fact is that an "n" was placed where the single quote mark is in the "original" spelling, because the letter that was once there has no English letter equivalent. However, the non-existent letter symbolized by " "", was spoken like an English "n", hence Dziewiencki. The current spelling of Devinki may first have appeared in print here in America when Kaileh's son, Efrayim (Froyim) Dziewiencki, signed a Social Security application as Fred Devinki. Oddly enough, on that same form, Kaileh is identified as Lola. We may never know why that was.

Ours was not the only Dziewiencki family in Wodzislaw. The family headed by Henoch Dziewiencki, unrelated to us, was known as the "furrier Dziewienckis," as they were engaged in the fur business, although they did not manufacture fur coats. It is also true that the Dziewiencki name is not exclusive to Jews. Sam's mother, Malka, known as "Maria" Devinki, remembers a gentile sawmill owner named Dziewiencki in the nearby town of Sedziszow.

But we are moving too far ahead of ourselves here. Even though we agreed to begin in earnest with the third generation - when Moshe Dziewiencki met Kaileh Jachimowiecz, and Shlomo Braun met Rivka

Rosenberg - we must take a quick step back a generation, to their parents, to properly set the stage.

Shlomo Braun was born to David and Aidl (maiden name Weinreich) Braun. According to Maria Devinki, David Braun was either the son or brother of a great rabbinic scholar, Schmuel Brenner. David Braun was also a great writer. Not in the subjective sense of a great story teller or novelist, but in the objective sense of writing like a calligrapher. Calligraphy was not David's profession, nor a hobby, he just had really great handwriting. "If you would see how my grandfather, his handwriting, you wouldn't believe in your life," said Maria. "With his everyday script, he could have written the Declaration of Independence," declared Sam Devinki.

Maria's mother, Rivka Rosenberg, came from a wealthy family. She was the daughter of Berish Rosenberg and Malka Szlanski, (Malka was also known as "Maria"). Malka's father was Kalman Szlanski and at the turn of the 20th century in Wodzislaw, Poland, Kalman meant business. He made his family's fortune in real estate. Originally, by acquiring the estates and properties of local land owners and Polish nobility. Before he was through, some said Kalman Szlanski owned half the whole town. Whatever the actual percentage, he owned entire streets and all the buildings on them. "And then, of course, when he passed away, everything was split for the children. He had nine children. So everybody had a house," said Maria. Accordingly, most of his direct and extended family lived in homes he owned.

Maria lived in one of five family homes in a row. On one side of the Braun's were Maria's grandfather, Berish Rosenberg, his second wife Feygeh and their daughters. On the other side was an aunt, Sarah Gitl Braun, who married Miago Szlanski. Then the parents of Calma Fienrise. And then Salchem Weingold.

City Hall was built on Szlanski land. The police station was on his land. Even the Jewish community headquarters, the "gemeinde," was his, until he sold it to the city. In fact, from a 2006 trip to Wodzislaw,

Sam Devinki learned that the "Gmina Wodzislaw" building still stands at number 6 and 8 "ill. Krakowska," or Krakowska St. It now houses a cooperative bank and the Vital Records Office. The police station, or "Komisariat policji," is right across the street.

We don't know much about Kaileh Jachimowiecz's parents beyond their names; her mother, Pola, known as "Perl" (maiden name, Berger) and her father, Chayim Jachimowiecz. Nor do we know much about Moshe Dziewiencki's mother other than her first name, Gitl. But we do know quite a bit about Moshe's father, Yosef Ha-Kohen Dziewiencki. Yosef was the "dyan" of the local Jewish community and *"gabbai"* of the Wodzislaw synagogue for 30-40 years.

The gabbai traditionally managed the synagogue proper and the people who worked there, as well as being the authority in charge of assigning ritual duties and honors for religious services. The gabbai was also traditionally charged with the collection and distribution of charitable giving funds. But his import didn't end there.

Dissecting his name, Yosef Ha-Kohen Dziewiencki, *Ha-kohen,* is the Hebrew name given to denote the lineage of a male descended from the ancient priestly class of Israel. That name, or title, *Ha-kohen,* literally, "the priest," is passed down the family tree from father to son. Historically, tribal divisions dominated specific regions of the Land of Israel, and the priests, as a class, represented a segment of the tribe of Levi. In the days of the Temple in Jerusalem, the Ha-kohen were in charge of all ritual functions, especially the intricate system of sacrifices. And although the Temple has lain in ruins for centuries and Judaism's religious structure has changed in practice, the descendants of this priestly class continue to maintain a unique identity within the Jewish religious community. Outside the work of the Temple, their main functions were as teachers and judges.

One thing the Ha-Kohen did *not* have, however, was hereditary rights to land, as most other Jews did have.

While publically and properly Yosef Ha-Kohen Dziewiencki, he was also known as Yosl Flam. "Yosl" being a Yiddish form of the Hebrew name "Yosef." And "Flam" being the Yiddish word for "flame." In Yosl's case, "flam" referred to the flaming-red birthmark prominently emblazoned on his face.

In short, at the time Sam Devinki's grandparents met and wed, his great-grandparents were the pillars and leaders of the Wodzislaw business and religious communities. Consequently, the arranged marriages of Sam's grandparents - of Moshe Dziewiencki to Kaileh Jachimowiecz, and of Shlomo Braun to Rivka Rosenberg - represented a major "merger" in Wodzislaw social circles.

Rivka Rosenberg, (also known as "Regina"), was born July 1, 1892; the eldest of Berish and Malka "Maria" Rosenberg's two children. Rivka and her brother, David, had four step siblings - in birth order, Yaacov, Hindeh, Blumeh and Yehudis - from Berish Rosenberg's second marriage to Feygeh Miriam. Incidentally, "Berish" is a variation of the Yiddish name, "Ber," which means "bear" in English, just like it sounds. The Hebrew equivalent of Berish is "Dov," with "Bernard" being the Polish variation.

Rivka Rosenberg would marry Shlomo Braun; the eldest of five children born to David and Aidl (maiden name, Weinreich) Braun. Shlomo's four siblings, coming after him in birth order, were Yosef, Moshe, Noach and Sarah Gitl.

In 1932, a tragic freak family accident resulted in the death of Moshe's six-year-old daughter, Esther. As it happened, Moshe Braun's house sat high atop a hill. One day, brother Noach was coming to the house for what were reportedly frequent visits. When little Esther saw her Uncle Noach approaching, she enthusiastically leaned out an upstairs window to greet him, lost her balance and fell to her death down the side of the hill. Esther is buried in the Jewish cemetery in Wodzislaw.

Shlomo Braun, which would be "Solomon," in Polish, was born in Hannover, Germany. He moved to Wodzislaw and met Rivka. They were married there, but men moved back to Hannover where their first two children, David Leyzer and Malka "Maria" Chana, were born. Their third child, Shmuel Yitzhak, was born shortly after their return to Wodzislaw.

Shlomo Braun was a "Pitshover hasid" and a member of "Agudat Yisreal." Following World War I, in which he served, Shlomo and Rivka moved to Hannover, Germany and began a business selling military surplus items. They later moved to Wodzislaw, Poland, where they established, built and ran a large-scale wholesale import-export business with a fleet of trucks that distributed products throughout Poland. They dealt in farm products such as watermelons and grapes, chocolate, coffee, coal and fuel oil. They sometimes shipped meat as well, often coordinating those shipments to coincide with shipments of blocks of ice to neighboring towns. But their primary business, and the reason they got the trucks in the first place, was making shipments of feathers to the bedding industry. Those feathers were often trucked to the Baltic, then shipped overseas to Sweden, Montreal, Canada and Chicago here in the U.S.

Taking advantage of every opportunity to prosper, between shipments, when the Braun's fleet would otherwise sit idle, the trucks were rented out to others; however many "others" it took to load each truck as fully as could be.

As a place to gather goods for shipment, Shlomo also owned a large warehouse. With a mass of inventory behind her, quite literally, Rivka opened and operated a retail store front from which dry goods, groceries, cigarettes, etc. were sold, as well as a restaurant of sorts, selling coffee, tea, cakes, cookies and other foods primarily for the truckers who came there for goods.

******

On the other side of the family, Kaileh Jachimowiecz was the eldest of six children born to Pola "Perl" (Berger) and Chayim Jachimowiecz. Her name, "Kaileh," was pronounced "ky-leh" in the dialect of Polish Jews. Her siblings, in birth order following Kaileh, were Shmuel Harsh, Yaacov (known as "Yankl"), Moshe, Aharon (later changed to Aaron Jacomowitz), and Mordechai (later changed to Max Jacomowitz).

Kaileh Jachimowiecz would marry Moshe Dziewiencki. Moshe was the ninth of nine children born to Yosef Ha-Kohen Dziewiencki and his wife Gitl. Leading up to Moshe, in birth order from oldest to second youngest, were his eight siblings; Pinchas, Nuchem, Rivka, Rachel, Zlateh, Etl, Rachl and Manyeh.

From 1896 to 1914, Moshe and Kaileh would have seven children; Shmuel Hirsh, Riftsheh, Yankl, Fatl, Chayim (later changed to Henry Jevinsky), Pola and Efrayim (known as "Froyim," later changed to "Fred Devinki"). When Moshe died in 1918, Kaileh went to live with their eldest son, Shmuel Hirsh Dziewiencki, his wife, Eter Tzipeh (maiden name, Mine), and their two children, Moshe and Franyeh-Fradl.

Four of the five Dziewiencki brothers, in birth order, Shmuel Hirsh, Yankl, Chayim and

Efrayim (Fred), ran a textile business before the war. Their father, Moshe, began the business in his home town of Lodz, a textile center, when he was still a teenager. Moshe's father passed away there when Moshe was 14 or 15, meaning Moshe had to start something of his own. By 1920, he was moving textiles to Wodzislaw, his mother's home town, and when Moshe married Kaileh, they moved to Wodzislaw, set up a store and started their family.

Moshe passed away from an illness in 1918, when Fred, the youngest child, was 4 years old. Shmuel and Chayim were left mainly in charge. Their mother Kaileh, was sickly and was accordingly not involved with the business.

Shmuel Hirsh married Ester Tzipeh Mine; a woman from Dzialoszyce. They had two children. A son, Moshe (who later became Morris Devon) and a daughter, Franyeh-Fradl.

Moshe (later Morris), survived and is living in Toronto. But both parents and the daughter perished in the Holocaust.

The second oldest brother, Yankl Jachimowiecz married Pola Zalcman and had two children; Jadzia and Moshe. All were killed by the Germans when they were found hiding in a bunker.

Chayim (later Henry Jevinsky) married Esther Cukierand and had two children; Mania and Max. Chayim, Esther and Mania survived the war. Max was born after the war. They lived in Tel Aviv, Israel from 1975-1994, then came to the United States. First to New York and then to Kansas City, Missouri.

Brother Fatl was not involved with the textile business. He was a philosopher. He married Bracha Frohman shortly before the war. They and their infant daughter all perished in the Holocaust.

Riftsheh, known as Rivka, the eldest daughter, married Shmuel Hirsh

Jachimowiecz and had four children; Pola, Moshe, Gutsheh and Bibula. Maria believes one of the brothers is living in Israel at this writing, (2009).

The youngest daughter, Pola, married her first cousin, Shileib Rubinek and had two boys; Alek and Moshe (Moniek). Shileib perished in the Holocaust and Pola remarried David Eisenberg. It was the second marriage for them both.. Eisenberg's first wife and two children also perished in the Holocaust. Pola and David had one child together, Max Joseph Eisenberg, who resides in Los Angeles.

And with that, we come to focus on the parents of Sam Devinki; on the life and times of Efrayim "Froyim" Dziewiencki, later Fred Devinki and Malka or "Mala," finally, "Maria" Chana Braun.

******

Maria Braun was born June 1,1920 in Hannover, Germany to Shlomo and Rivka Braun. As a soldier in World War I, Shlomo suffered injuries so severe that he spent two years in a hospital recuperating. When he regained his health, when he was back on his feet again, he headed for Hannover, Germany. After a short time there, he started an army surplus business; uniforms, guns and other surplus war items.

Originally from Wodzislaw, Shlomo was making the trip back and forth from Hannover to Wodzislaw, a distance of roughly 800 kilometers, about 500 miles, for both businesses and personal reasons. It was around this time that he and Rivka were married. They eventually settled in Wodzislaw around 1924, when Maria was about four years old.

According to Maria, her father's family "got down to business" quite literally. Shlomo's father, David Braun, and apparently some, if not all four siblings, were in the feather business. They gathered goose down and feathers from area farmers and organized shipments to cities throughout Poland, in Germany, Sweden and Czechoslovakia, and even to Montreal, Canada, and Chicago, Illinois in the United States.

When Maria, her mother and husband moved to Kansas City, she used shipping manifests from 1939 to look for money owed to her family from before the war. She found some of that money, too, and she put it to very good use. But that story comes later.

Shipping feathers was only one part of the Braun operation in 1920's Poland. Because they owned the trucks they used to ship their company's main commodity, they also had a marketable commodity in the trucks themselves. The same kind of truck that snipped feathers could ship other goods, too, and since shipments of feathers went out only every few days, on other days, the Braun's rented space on their trucks to other businesses in need of that service, to make more of their fleet more profitable more of the time.

Live sheep and cattle were shipped to Sosnowiec, a city of about 130,000 in the late 1930s, with a Jewish population around 28,000. They also shipped butchered meat, planning those shipments out in advance to coincide with shipments of block ice to keep the fresh meat from spoiling on its overland journey.

Their business practices of the 1920s and '30s are still followed by modern moving van companies today. This was not a "U-Haul" operation. The Braun's trucks came with the Braun's own employees as drivers; "chauffeurs," said Maria, "we call it a chauffeur."

Also like moving van companies of today, the Braun's did what they could to make every truck load count. If a company had enough goods to fill an entire truck, so be it. They could rent the whole thing. But if a company only had enough goods to fill half the truck, or a third, or a quarter of the truck, the Braun's were only too happy to accommodate.

"We split them three or four ways," or however many ways it took, said Maria.

Maria's mother Rivka also sold goods more directly from a storefront in the warehouse where the goods and trucks were stored, selling both at the retail and wholesale levels. On a visit to Wodzislaw in October of 2006, Sam Devinki saw actual pages from the mid-1930's ledger of his father's store in the town library. The store's major buyers were registered there with their purchases, either individual customers buying at retail rates, or other businesses buying goods wholesale.

There is video footage of the librarian showing Sam how, on the left side of the ledger are purchases made by the store, and on the right are sales to the public; quite simply, accounts payable - accounts receivable.

Prosperous merchants, the family lived well and were well respected in Wodzislaw. They lived in a 200-year-old, 4,000 square foot house on the road from Krakow, "Krakow Street" as they called it, which served as the main street in Wodzislaw. The Braun's home was originally owned by Maria's maternal grandfather, Kalman Szlanski and stood right across the street from the City Hall of Gmina Wodzislaw, which also stood on land owned by Kalman Szlanski. As Maria recalls it, "my grandfather left a whole block of homes on this street."

This very old house had very modern conveniences. It had running water and indoor plumbing. As a "home entertainment system," the Braun's had a big console radio in one room, as well as a smaller radio that Maria said she and her schoolmates played while doing their homework around the big kitchen table, just like students today.

"We were civilized people!," said Maria. "Do you know that Europe was more civilized than any part of the world? Especially Germany, Austria, Sweden, Switzerland. Things where America didn't even know how to do it, we did it there. We were Europe!"

Maria and her two brothers - David Leyzer, 2 years older, and Shmuel Yitzhak, 5 years younger than Maria - each had their own room. The Braun's had live-in servants who did much of the house cleaning, laundry and childcare, but their mother Rivka "Regina," did the cooking.

"My mother cooked," said Maria. "The lady could help. She could peel things. She could cut up things. She could grind the beans. She could wash the dishes, but she didn't cook. My mother cooked. The only thing I can say and be honest with you, (in 1930's Wodzislaw), the food was a lot better than the food here, (in 2009 Kansas City). Because everything was natural. The hamburger was meat. The chicken was real chicken. Nothing was done by shots and by chemicals. Everything was natural."

Saturday, the rules of the Sabbath were very strictly adhered to. The entire family went to Shule from 8:00 or 8:30 in the morning until about 1:00 in the afternoon. After which, they all went home and had lunch. The whole family. The holy day was to be spent simply and solely enjoying the Sabbath. Jewish businesses were not allowed to open. Children were not allowed to do homework. If you wanted something to read, you could read something from the Bible.

Sam Devinki's cousin, Morris (Moshe) Devon recalls the ritual reminders to Jewish

businesses that came at the end of each business week. "We have to close Friday evening before Shabbos," Morris recalled in an interview in Kansas City in the fall of 2009. "So, there was a special guy that came, a guy with a hammer and he banged the door. He was from the Rabbinet. When he gave a bang, people know it's time to close. For sometimes Shabbos came earlier, sometime later. In the winter it comes earlier, in the summer it comes later. So he went around once and if you didn't close, he came around again. And again, he banged again on the door with a hammer. People were told, 'You have to close.' And they close. We had to close. It's Shabbos. As long as it's Shabbos, all the stores have to be closed. You couldn't buy nothing. All closed. Well, you could buy from the Polacks. The Polacks were open. But most of the businesses in the city were run by Jews.* And the Jewish people? All closed."

Morris was born in Wozislaw on August 4, 1929. Orphaned in the Holocaust, the Canadian Jewish Congress, who took in war orphans under the age of 18 from Poland,

Germany and France, moved Morris to Toronto where he has lived for the last 62 years, (as of 2009), working as a clothing designer.

*(According to Morris Devon, the fact that Jews ran most of the businesses in town was something the Polish community frequently and sometimes loudly complained about.)

During the week, by law, the children all went to school. Parents were charged with initially enrolling their children between the ages of 5 and 7. In the morning, from 8:00 a.m. to 3:00 p.m., they went to the public school. Then, in the afternoon and early evening, from 3:30 to 6:30 p.m., some of the Jewish children attended the Hebrew school, "Bias Yaakov," the "House of Jacob" for religious instruction.

The right and responsibility of educating their children came early to Jews in Poland. The ruling Polish nobles granted them self-government in the "Charter of Jewish Liberties," in the year 1264. That charter gave the Jewish community exclusive jurisdiction over religious and cultural issues, as well as the education of their children. Children 4-8 years old learned Hebrew and Yiddish. Children 8-13 years old studied the Talmud.

By the early 1900s in Wodzislaw, the educational curriculum had expanded to include subjects commonly studied by students the world over today; history, math, geography. Every citizen was required to finish seven grades of formal education. For that formal education, students would attend the public Polish, sometimes called the "Catholic" school that served both Christian and Jewish students. While there was religious insulation from Christianity within the community, it was not through physical isolation from Christians. The Christian and Jewish communities educated their children together.

Along with formal classes on the main curriculum subjects students study in school today, they also went on field trips, just like kids today. Maria recalled a trip to Krakow, "the most beautiful, historic city in Poland," said Maria, about 35 miles from Wodzislaw.

As part of the history lesson learned in Krakow, Maria's class went to visit the tombs of Polish nobility enshrined there. "They have all the Kings and all the Queens buried in Krakow. They were not buried, (in cemeteries). They were buried in tombs standing up. And their crowns were still on each one, the gold crowns. And it's a glass casket. You see all the beautiful jewelry that they have.

"Matter of fact, when Hitler came he tried to open these tombs and take out a lot of stuff, and there was a big, big fight with the religious leaders, Catholic and Polish Catholic, not to touch them, (said as if saying 'toe-shhh dem')."

Beyond math and history, Maria was also interested in geography and art. Two things she soon combined to form a business. Maria knew the surrounding countries fairly well, a lot about Poland, and quite a bit about her native Germany. She also had some artistic talent; an ability to draw. And it was that combination of knowledge and talent that allowed her to make a little money.

At home, after school one day, Maria sketched a map of North America just for fun. She sketched other continents and countries they were studying as well. These caught the eye of other students and soon she was making hand drawn atlases and selling them to fellow students for five 'zlotys'. At that time, five zlotys was equal to about one dollar.

As a form of currency, the zloty dates back to the Middle Ages and is still the official currency of Poland. Pronounced "zwalta", the literal translation is "golden." In fact, the term was first used in the 14th century to refer to any one of a number of foreign gold coins, like German doucats. But in 1496, "the zloty," as a single specific coin, was approved as the Polish national currency. One zloty was the monetary equivalent of 30 groszy, (the groszy, as a coin, had been around since 1347). The modern zloty is made up of 100 groszy.

Maria also managed to sell school supplies. Things like books, pens and pencils, even school uniforms. At the age of about 16, Maria said she was checking prices for such items all over town; buying them for a little less, selling them to her schoolmates for a little more. And while she may not have earned much in dollars and cents, (or in her case, zloty and groszy), what she did earn was the good sense to buy a thing "for a little less" and sell it for a little more, and *that* was priceless.

Young people in Europe lived within well developed, socially accepted guidelines. Marriages were arranged. It was ultimately up to parents to negotiate who their son or daughter would spend the rest of their lives with. It was forbidden for young girls to go out unescorted, and nothing was "co-educational."

"Oh, times were very strict. We never mixed with boys. Girls were one side sitting. The boys were the other side," said Maria. But, "it was not so restrictive that we had no life, don't get yourself wrong. It's very, very, very religious, but we live a life; the kids have a life. We didn't have to go around always with the parents."

For instance, there were movie theaters in town and they periodically went to see shows unescorted. Maria's crowd of Jewish and non-Jewish girl friends would sometimes even take a bus to a theater in a bigger city, as long as they were home at a reasonable hour.

Morris Devon recalled seeing his first movie on a sheet on the wall of the fire department. "The whole city came, everybody came, because it was something new. We never seen a movie in our life! I must have been about 8- 9 years old," said Morris. He even recalls the movie they saw. "I remember Mickey Rooney. He played in a movie, 'Miasto Chlopcow'. In Polish, it's mean, 'the city from boys.'" In English, "Boys Town".

As Maria said, the people of Wodzislaw lived, learned, worked and played together. The social divisions were mainly along economic lines, rather than by religion or heritage. For example, the Braun's were very good friends with the gentile "Burgomaster," or Mayor and his family. They lived right across the street from one another. The Mayor's sister-in-law was one of Maria's best friends. And Maria herself made an entire outfit for the Mayor's wife.

"So, I was a very talented girl," said Maria. "Give myself credit, what can I do? I crocheted the Mayor's wife a dress and a coat; a blue dress and a white coat. Took me three months to make this. And I made it, and she was the belle of the evening!"

After completing his required seven years of public education, Maria's older brother David went to religious school, the sheeva. David was 21 and employed as a bookkeeper for a large farm hardware business when World War II broke out. Maria's younger brother, Shmuel, did finish his required public seven years, but he was 14 years old at the start of the war. As Maria put it, "He didn't have enough time to survive to go to higher grades."

After finishing her initial seven years of education, Maria planned to continue her studies in hopes of becoming a mathematics teacher. She was 18 in June of 1938, when she enrolled at the "Gimnasium," a three year, co-ed college, in Jedrezow, about 10 miles from Wodzislaw. Maria lived in a dorm there during the week, coming home to Wodzislaw Fridays after class for the weekends.

She signed up for a second year of classes the following June of 1939, but would never finish that year or even that semester, never finish her formal education, never become the math teacher she dreamed of being.

That following September, a month before first semester classes ended, World War II began. The end of a dream. The beginning of a nightmare.

******

Part 2:

The War Years

Maria Braun recalled a conversation in her home with her parents one afternoon, in the Spring of 1939. After learning in school about the German assault on Czechoslovakia, she and other students were wondering if that would be the end of their aggression or if there would be a larger conflict. Her father told what he remembered about the start of World War I and warned Maria and the rest of the family that if there was to be a broader conflict, they would need to prepare for big, big changes in the country.

Maria recalled that conversation, and how right her father had been when, the following September 1, the German army rolled into Poland and would soon take control of Wodzislaw. From that day on, everything changed. They cut the beards of many Jews. Jewish businesses were taken over and given to Poles. Many were sent to forced labor camps and weapons manufacturing plants. There were random killings.

"My friends, the closest friends, where we attended school all through the years, they're non-Jewish, were afraid to be any longer close with us. They tried to separate themselves," said Maria. "We felt like we (hadn't) done anything wrong. We were not changed. We are the same people. What happened? We were too young to understand this."

This scenario had played itself out initially the year before in Germany and Austria when Hitler Youth, the Gestapo and the German SS ransacked thousands of Jewish homes and businesses, destroyed some 267 synagogues, murdered nearly 100 Jews, and arrested another 25,000-30,000 Jews and sent them to concentration camps. This all happened on November 9th & 10th, 1938, the "Kristallnacht," or "Crystal Night," "The Night of Broken Glass," that was triggered by the assassination in Paris of German diplomat Ernst vom Rath by a German-born Polish Jew by the name of Herschel Grynszpan.

While this established the German game plan for Poland, many historians believe plans for such a "pogrom," an organized persecution and/or massacre of a minority group, had been in the making for at least a year prior to Kristallnacht. Adolf Hitler had come to power as Chancellor of Germany in January of 1933. That very year, the German Jews who had been fully integrated into all levels of the business, social and military communities became targets of laws restricting their citizenship, their ability to earn a living and their access to education. While Jews made up less than 1 percent of the total population, Hitler's government propaganda portrayed the Jews as being responsible for Germany's loss in World War I and the hyper-inflation and economic collapse mat followed. Such historians say the assassination of Ernst vom Rath merely provided the opportunity, not the motive, to carry out their anti-Semitic plans.

In hind sight, Maria believes her small town was not "sophisticated" enough to have heard enough details of that horrible night, and all that led up to it, to fully appreciate that the same thing might happen to them. "So to us, it was a shock," said Maria. She was very surprised at how swiftly her former gentile Polish friends and customers distanced themselves from her and

her family, "but we were doing our best to continue to operate the business 'til the German army came in and cleaned everything out."

The business was a shipping, trucking, import-export operation Maria's father, Shlomo, ran in partnership with a non-Jew, Jusick Gondorowicz. Shlomo and Jusick had known each other as friends. They lived in the same neighborhod. They had served together in World War I. Jusick had become an officer in the Polish Army, a position that had helped the two partners obtain the necessary licenses for their exporting business.

Maria recalls a conversation where the two men were talking about Poland preparing for the impending threat of a German invasion. Jusick, confident of the Polish Army's fighting ability, said, "We are so strong, we are not going to lose a button from our uniform!" Shlomo jokingly answered that with, "Not only will you lose a button, you'll lose the whole uniform!"

It was about a week later, on Friday, September 1, 1939, that the German Army rolled into Wodzislaw. Maria remembers them riding into town, led by German soldiers on motorcyles with sidecars. The soldiers in the sidecars were indiscriminantly shooting and killing people as they came. Maria personally saw one man shot and killed on the sidewalk in front of their store. At the outbreak of the war, 2,400 Jews lived in Wodzislaw. Rumor had it that 100 of them were shot and killed that first day.

Maria's future husband, Efrayim (Froyim) Dziewiencki, (later Fred Devinki), was among those shot that day. Their son, Sam, grew up seeing the long, uneven, horizontal scar attesting to it. As Sam relates the story his father told, a soldier had fired at Fred from the road, as

Fred walked across a farm field. The bullet ripped through him, slicing across his stomach, splitting him open. Fred grasped his wound and fell to the ground. And then, according to Fred, an "act of G-d" occurred. The German soldiers got out to enter the field where Fred lay bleeding, to see if he was dead or to finish him off if need be. And as they did, the heavens opened up and the rain came down in sheets. That deluge changed their minds. The soldiers decided to get back in their vehicle, to get out of the rain, to go on their way, and to leave young Froyim Dziewiencki to whatever fate awaited him.

As fate would have it, a farmer found him lying in that field. Seriously injured, but very much alive. Fred asked to be taken to a hospital in a neighboring town. They went there by horse and buggy, about 15 miles away.

Fred had told the farmer he had family there, but in truth, the family he knew there was that of his former fiancee. An engagement that had been called off when Fred set his sights on Maria Braun. Fred was at least still friends with her brothers.

His injury, recovery and general wariness, kept Fred away from Wodzislaw for over a year. As the Germans into Wodzislaw, they spread throughout the town, taking over the police station early on. Most of the Polish police officers were dismissed, but a few were kept on staff as advisors, especially the "folks deutsche," who spoke German, to act as interpreters and communicate with the Polish citizens. The police and the Germans were also the only members of the community to carry guns. The general public did not own firearms.

As Maria recalls it, roughly three months after the army first took control of Wodzislaw, sometime just before Christmas, 1939, the army came back into town to confiscate goods from Jewish businesses. "They come with trucks and they needed all type of merchandise," said Maria. "Whatever a merchant had on hand, they took out from the store and they didn't even say, 'thank you.' They just loaded it up."

The Braun's did not know that the German's had established the practice of taking what they wanted without giving a dime, or a "szloty," for it. So they argued with the men taking goods from their store. Coffee and tea were very expensive items at that time and the store sold them in bulk. Maria's mother, Rivka wanted to save a small portion of the coffee being taken. "She want to take a little bit away, to save for us," but a soldier that Maria now assumes was a member of the Gestapo, leveled his gun and told her mother, "Stay away. Don't touch it."

Maria wanted to know why.

"One of the Gestapo - he must probably be Gestapo, at that time I didn't know too much about Gestapo, he was in the black uniform -1 stood in front of him, I said, 'Why don't you let her take it?' I spoke good German. 'Why don't you let her take this? It's for the children?'

"He give me two slaps on my face with a leather (crop). For days I had lines here. It's just like he cut it in. And after this, we really didn't have too much left." Or so it seemed at the time. "After a while, they decided we lived in too good of a neighborhood."

Within that next year, the local police "advisors" kept on by the Germans, had helped advise them about people in the town; like which familes were Jewish, and of the Jews, which families were rich and which were poor. Thereby organizing the neighborhoods for the next big move.

In January of 1940, the Nazis established a ghetto in Wodzislaw. Into it they forced the relocation of Jews from Wodzislaw, the neighboring city of Jedrzejow, the distant cities of Ciecho-cinek and Lodz, and the district of Poznan. There were 200 dwellings with about 600 rooms. Most of the buildings in the ghetto were small huts made of wood and mud. By June of 1941, there were 3,315 Jews in the Wodzislaw ghetto, including 1,831 refugees. By June of '42, the number had risen to 3,837. People were made to live together sometimes seven to a room in two-room apartments.

For the first 3-4 months of 1940, many of the young men of the town, mostly those 16-25 years of age, were sent to Sedziszow, a railroad station, to work on the tracks. Later on, they were made to work laying stones to pave the streets of Wodzislaw. Others worked locally, cleaning houses and taking care of the sick. Maria was part of a crew of young men and women made to line the banks of a river with stones. She remembers riding there on her bicycle with a group of 10-15 girls.

This went on for several months, until the beginning of 1941, when German soldiers began taking men away in trucks to camps making munitions and petroleum for the German war machine. Maria's brothers, David and Schmuel were among those taken. Where they went, no one knew. It was later discovered that her brothers had been taken to the Skarzysko-Kamiena work camp. It was not a death camp. Maria saw Schmuel about six months later. He had run away from the camp. Her brother David she would not see for the next two years, until near the end of 1943, when they were reunited in hiding.

Typhus hit Wodzislaw in 1941. A bacterial infection most often seen in areas of poor hygiene and cold weather, typhus is most often spread by exposure to the lice, fleas and feces of rats. Victims often experience a dry, hacking cough, chills, back and abdominal pain, severe muscle and joint pain, high and prolonged fever -104 degrees and above for up to two weeks -headaches, nausea, vomiting and a deep red rash that begins on the chest, then spreads over nearly the entire body. Only the palms of the hands and soles of the feet remain unscathed.

Those who came down with typhus were taken to the ghetto. "They cut off the ghetto from the city, and put all the sick people in the ghetto along with the well ones!," said Maria.

The presiding Kreishauptmann, or administrator, gave the order to vaccinate Jews in the ghetto against typhus in August of '41. However, Maria said, "They (the Germans) was afraid to go near there. They would have come in and kill 'em, but they was afraid if they go in that section, they might get sick with the typhus. So they assigned us to go in."

The "us," in this case, was a group of nine young girls, including Maria, friends who had been students together, were assigned and trained to care for the typhus patients, as well as the victims.

"We have to go every morning to wash them, change them, feed them - if any food was ₜ available. Some died. Some were killed and, naturally, we had to bury them," said Maria. "That went on for two to three months. And when we were through with this, every Friday night, they (the Germans) went to another house and took out one of those girls. Saturday morning, we heard so-and-so was killed, right in front of her house! The next Friday night they did this to another one. Eight of them, all eight of them I lost. I was the only one left.

"I was the only one left, so I decided I'm not going be here too much longer because maybe next Friday, it's time for me. So, I went into hiding. I had a friend, a non-Jewish friend and he made me papers. I had long blond hair with those little, what-do-you-call-it, braids and very tiny. I didn't look very Jewish. He made me papers and I had the Red Cross badge and papers (from caring for the typhus patients). So when I was wearing my Jewish band, the Mogan David, I wore the Red Cross badge on top of it. And that's why I could go out in places where they didn't know me well, (outside the ghetto) and buy food or exchange for something, or work for somebody, even clean a house or cook to bring something home for my parents."

Then she made a bigger move. Maria went to Krakow. There, with papers declaring her a non-Jewish person, she worked in a restaurant and in a hospital.

After a time working in Krakow, Maria wanted to return to Wodzislaw. She knew her brothers were no longer there, but she began to fear what might have happened to her parents. In a very bold move, she hitched a ride home on a German truck. The Germans drove her all the way there, not knowing she was Jewish.

When Maria got back to Wodzislaw, "it was quiet. There were no more young people my age any longer there. The majority were already sent out to all kinds of work. Whatever was left, a few men, all the younger ones, they took back to that railroad station and I was one of them. I worked there, until 1942."

At that time, there were armed guards who controlled the ghetto; the "Jewish police" they were called, "and they gave the information to us: What to do. Where to live, and when they needed us. And one particular night," said Maria, "one of those policemen said, 'there's going to be a clean up, completely.'" An "Aussieger," they called it, a plan to "clean out" the older generation.

One day in 1942, the Germans came in trucks and took away as many Jews as they could, which was not unusual. "We thought all those people were going to work and that they would come back the next week, or next month, or whatever," Maria said. Only this time, the trucks were not taking the people to work. They were taking them to their deaths. No one who got on those trucks ever returned.

Maria's grandfather, Berish Rosenberg, was supposed to get on one of those trucks, but he had the temerity to ask, "Why? What were they doing? Where were they going?" - For questioning their authority, her grandfather Berish was shot and killed on the spot.

That same day, a Sunday, Yom Kippur of 1942, family members and friends of Froyim (Fred) Dziewiencki's were discovered hiding in a basement in the Zalcman house. Pola Zalcman was married to Fred's brother Yankl. Yankl and Pola had two children; Jadzia and Moshe. The Zalcman's were a wealthy family in town. They ran the local flour mill. There was a storage room under the house where they kept bags of flour. They thought no one would think to look for them there.

Fred's mother Kaileh, his sister Rivka, his brother-in-law Shmuel Hersh Jachimowiecz and others hiding there were all taken to the Wodzislaw cemetery. They were shot and killed there. In all, 36 Jews were killed there that day and buried in one mass grave.

It was later discovered that a Polish policeman by the name of Miechowski told the Gestapo that there were Jews hiding beneath the Zalcman house. After the war, Miechowski returned to Wodzislaw where he was recognized as someone who had a hand in killing local Jews. The Russians, in charge of the city at the time, put him on trial. Sam Devinki's cousin, Kalmen Feinreisen, testified against Miechowski, naming those he had helped kill. Miechowski was hanged for his crimes.

All told, the Nazis transported about 3,000 Jews from the Wodzislaw ghetto to Treblinka; the extermination camp where Maria's father, Solomon Braun, was sent to his death in 1941. On or about September 20,1942, the Nazis would liquidate the Wodzislaw ghetto altogether. Those remaining were gathered into the market square and marched about 175 km, about 110 miles, NE to Sedziszow. Those who could not keep up were shot en route. The Szczekociny ghetto was also closed with their people marched about 22 km, about

15 miles, east to Sedziszow. When they got there, Sedziszow was being liquidated as well. That night, the old and sick were shot in the same meadow where the rest were camped for the night, and in the morning, those still alive were put on trains to Treblinka.

Maria Braun, her mother Rivka and Froyam (Fred) Dziewiencki would not be among them. It was just before that final, fateful September transport that they planned and made good their escape into hiding. Several member of Fred's family - his brothers Chayim, Yankl and Fatl, and members of their families - escaped separately into hiding.

Fred's brother Chayim, (later Henry Jevinsky), his wife Esther (Cukier), their daughter Mania and Chayim's nephew, Moshe Dziewiencki, (later Morris Devon), who would have been 10 or 12 at the time, survived in hiding on a farm. (Interviewed for this account, Moshe, later Morris, was uncertain of his age at the time of the war because there was a discrepancy in his official birth records that variously showed his birth year as 1927 or '29.) Moshe's father, Shmuel Hersh, and his mother, Esther Tzipeh (Mine), had given Moshe to his Uncle Chayim when Shmuel and Esther were sent off to Treblinka. In the family pedigree, prepared by Phillip Applebaum, Esther is said generally to have "perished in the Holocaust." While Shmuel Hersh, more specifically, was said to have died "...as a slave laborer in the Nazi-run Skarzysko-Kamienna munitions factory, Skarzysko-Kamienna, Poland." Chayim and Esther Jevinsky later had a son, Max, in 1949, and emigrated to the United States in May of 1952.

Fred's brother Yankl, his wife, Pola (Zalcman), and their two children Jadzia and Moshe all perished in the Holocaust.

Fred's brother Fatl, his wife Bracha (Frohman) and their infant daughter also perished, but ironically, Fatl's baby girl may have saved Maria Braun's life. As Maria tells the story, before the final Aussieger, Fatl was in Russia, but the baby was still in Wodzislaw when the

Germans came with transports to take another group of Jews to the work camps. During the process of choosing who would go and who would stay, Maria was holding that baby. Because of that little bundle of protection, she was allowed to stay. Someone from Fatl's family came for the child the next day.

The homes of Jewish families were taken from them and given to others, mainly the Poles and Germans occupying the town. Maria and her mother were moved into the small apartment of a building janitor. While they were living there, a German soldier came to ask Maria to buy coffee for him. He knew of her connections from the family's previous wholesale business. Maria explained that her supplier was in Krakow. The soldier offered to take her there, if she would agree to buy him coffee. Maria explained that she had no way of knowing if her connection still existed, but that she was willing to go and see what she could do.

On the way, the soldier talked to Maria about the war, not as an enemy, but as a fellow human being. He said how sad he was to be away from his wife and children. How he was afraid for his family, not knowing how they were, if they had enough to eat. She recalled feeling sorry for him.

When Maria and the German soldier arrived in Krakow, they headed for the Jewish ghetto. She was to go in to see if the man she knew was still there, but before she got out of the car, she told the soldier, "Under one condition. You can kill me. You can do whatever you want, but I'm not going to risk my friends. I risk myself. If you let me go to that place where they live, if they are still alive, then I do my best to get you what you want. But if you want to go with me, you can kill me now." He let her go by herself.

When Maria was trained to care for the typhus patients, she was given the arm band of the Red Cross. She put on that arm band now.

Covering the blue band that marked her as a Jew. The band with the word Jude, German for Jew, at the center of a Mogan David. The ghetto was partitioned off with a short wall. There were two doors in the wall to enter through. Once inside, she switched the arm bands back and headed for the place she remembered going. It had been just 6 -8 short months, but in that time her whole world had changed.

She found the man on the third floor, just as she remembered and explained the situation. She told him, "I don't know what's going to happen, but I risk my life. He sounds to me like a human being, even though he's a German. He was so polite to me all through the trip."

So, Maria bought a 10 pound bag of coffee with the deutsche marks the soldier had given her. She even returned the soldier's change to him. She also told the soldier that was the last coffee the man had. This was not true, but Maria wanted to put an end to it. And she did. The soldier drove her home, dropped her off at the Wodzislaw ghetto and that was the last she saw of him.

As mentioned in Part 1 of this history, Maria once handmade a dress and coat for the wife of the gentile "Burgomaster," the town Mayor. The Mayor's wife was to wear them at a Christmas party. While Maria had crocheted the outfit itself, for the seams, she needed a sewing machine. And for that, since she was no longer living in her own home, able to use her own machine, she went to someone she knew in the ghetto who had a business making clothing in secret. He let Maria use his sewing machines.

It was around this time, mid-September, 1942, that Jusick Gondorowicz came to her one day to tell her that the Aussieger was coming, and that she needed to make plans to get away. Maria told Jusick there was no heed. That the Mayor's wife had offered her a place to hide with them in the event of an Aussieger.

As Maria recalls it, Jusick was aghast at this, saying, "That's the most dangerous place you could choose! Girl wake up! Do you understand where you are going? She is going to do this for pity, because of the things you do for her, but this is not a saving." Jusick was adamant, "Sunday, they

are having a Aussieger to clean up the city completely. And if you don't make up your mind what to do...."

She asked Jusick what she should do. He said he had already talked with a farmer about hiding Maria and her mother on his property. He had yet to make the final arrangements, but that they should make ready.

A day or two after that, Maria had another visitor. As she worked on that dress one night, someone knocked on the window. The man who ran the shop didn't know him and asked Maria, did she? She did. It was Fred.

Froyam "Fred" Dziewiencki had known Malka "Maria" Braun for a long time. Fred was a friend of Maria's older brother, David. "He (Fred) was six years older than I was," said Maria. But she had not seen him since before he was shot the day the Germans first rolled into town.

Maria felt something must be wrong. She opened the door. Fred told Maria, "You don't know what's going to happen. Sunday is going to be the Aussieger," the final transport of Wodzislaw Jews to Treblinka. It was to be on Yom Kippur, Sunday, September 20,1942. He had heard the news from a friend in the Polish police, who told him the police force was already prepared to help the Germans carry it out.

Fred also had plans to go into hiding in a bunker on a farm. However, he worried that if he went alone, the farmer would kill him and simply take his money. But that if he had Maria and her mother with him, then he felt the odds of survival for all of them would be greatly improved. And that if they were to go into hiding together,

Fred believed one more thing would help.

"He says, 'We have to get married,' said Maria.

"I said, 'What is the big deal now to get married? My father is not around anymore. My two

brothers are not around. What do I care if we get married?'

"He said, 'That's the safest! Because they say that younger married couples have a better chance

to survive than the single ones."

"I say, 'What kind of protection can you give me?' He's not a soldier!

"He says, 'I'm still a man. I still have more power than you, a girl; a school girl.'

"He told me, 'You're going to be by yourself. Your father's going to Treblinka. Your mother's

not young any more.' She was maybe late 40s or 50. And he says, 'What are you going to do?

You know what the soldiers will do to you?'

"When Fred told me this, he scared me to death. So, he said, 'The only choice we have is to get

married.'"

In 1940s Poland, this was not the way marriages happened. Marriages were arranged by the parents and followed a well defined set of social and religious mitzvah. A marriage arranged between the bride and groom themselves was well outside accepted social norms.

"So I asked my mother. I ask her, I said, 'So what should I do?'

"She said, 'I cannot tell you now. It's too late. It's a time that everyone has to decide by them-

self. Listen honey, you do the best you can. If you want to get married, get married. You have

somebody with you.'

"So I said, 'What's going to happen to you? Where are you going to go?'

"She said, 'What happens to me, don't worry about it. Yusik said he was going to have a place

for both of us, and I trust that he will do the best he can. You are young. I've already lived my

life, and I've had a family. So you decide.'"

Maria decided to marry Fred.

That decision made, they next had to decide how and where they would be wed, and by whom. There were only a few Jews still in town. Luckily, Maria had an uncle, a "Shoichet" who could perform the ceremony. A Shoichet is a butcher trained in the kosher slaughtering of meat. As such, a Shoichet had nearly the same social status as a Rabbi, able to perform a wedding or a bris. And with that authority, he could give them *Chuppah Kiddushin,* the marriage blessing. "So we went, it was a Thursday we went, to this Uncle of mine and explain to him the situation. And my uncle the Shoichet said, "I give you the blessing." On one condition: "I need a witness. I cannot give the blessing without the witness."

For a proper witness, Maria called upon a dear and prominent friend and neighbor, "who I went to school with," the sister-in-law of the Mayor, the Burgomaster. "The Mayor was living on that side, I was living on this side, on the same street. For years and years they knew my parents. We were good friends, and so I ask her. I said, 'will you go with me in the ghetto? I will protect you.' We were in the ghetto. We couldn't get out from the ghetto. And she went with me." This was on a Friday.

"She went with me and I told my uncle she was not Jewish. He says, 'She's human. She still is a human being.'"

In the meantime, Fred was out looking for a ring. He went and bought a ring for five zlotys and told some of his friends what he was about to do with it. Among the friends he told were two sisters, the Blooms, and their two boyfriends from Sosnowiec, who were brothers. They decided to get married along with Fred and Maria. And then, even one more couple. "That was Hanka Bi-adak's sister Cesia with Karol Vrona," Maria recalled.

Even more last minute than Fred and Maria, none of the other couples had a ring. So, to bless each marriage, the ring Fred bought was passed down the line from one hand to the next, to seal all the makeshift bonds of holy matrimony. Four couples in all were married that day with the very same ring. - Who ended up with that ring? Maria has no idea. But she does know that she and Fred, and Karol Vrona and his wife Hanka were the only ones to survive. The Bloom sisters and the brothers they married all perished in the Holocaust.

The next day, Saturday, Gondorowicz met with Maria again. She said she wasn't sure if she was going to go, because now there were three people. "Who's the third," he asked? "I said, 'Fred Dziewiencki.' He said, 'Where does he come in? Who is he to you?' I said, 'I married him yesterday.'"

At this point, Maria's brothers had been sent to the Skarzysko-Kamienna work camp. Maria's father, Shlomo, had been taken away and is believed to have been murdered at Treblinka death camp. Maria's mother, Rivka, received a letter informing her of Shlomo's death, allegedly from an undisclosed illness, along with a few of his personal effects. But they still did not want to believe the Aussieger would happen, and so prepared for Yom Kippur as best they could.

It was very soon after this that they went into hiding. The first place was the farm of Wladyslaw Chelowski. When they arrived there, in the back of a horse drawn wagon, under a load of hay, nothing had been prepared for them. So Fred and Chelowski chose a place on the barn floor and began to dig. They dug a pit in the ground that was roughly 15 feet long x 10 feet wide x 5 feet deep. Just under 5 feet tall herself, Maria could not stand upright. This would be "home" for the next two years.

Horse blankets were laid on the damp, dirt floor beneath them. By day they sat there in that hole, on those blankets. Boards covered them in, and hay covered the boards. At nigiht, some nights, when all was quiet, they could come out. They had a lamp, but there was no heat, no running water, no sanitation. At night they would go to the river nearby, perhaps half a mile away, to bathe in the middle of the night. From the river, they would also pull a bucket of water and that would be the water supply all three had for the next day.

They lived in the clothes they came in wearing. Although, over the time they were in hiding, Maria was still a growing girl and outgrew the shoes she walked in with. In the beginning, they were fed potatoes and bread. As time went on, they received less and would sometimes sneak out to steal an extra potato or two from what the farmer was feeding his pigs. The bread they got was the old, stale bread on the day the farmer's wife made fresh. "She (the farmer's wife) was very uncomfortable with us. She wanted to get rid of us. So she baked the bread Saturday and didn't give it to us 'til next Saturday. It was so hard that we couldn't chew it," Maria recalled. There were no fresh vegetables. No meat. No eggs. No milk. No cheese. Ever.

They hid there, in that hole in the ground, for 27 months. It must have seemed forever. Twice, while they were there, Gestapo agents came to search the farm, poking around the bam floor and into the piles of hay with their bayonets. If the point went through, they knew they'd found a hole, a possible hiding place. If the point met with solid resistance, they moved on. The boards over their bunker provided the protection they needed. Both times, the Gestapo moved on.

Fred, Maria and Rivka had left a large sum of money, perhaps hundreds of thousands of szlotys, in the care of Jusick Gondorowicz to pay the farmer. It had happened in other cases that the people hiding Jews would take their money and then turn them in to the Gestapo or other authorities, saying they had been robbed by Jews who were still on their property. Those Jews would be killed.

To keep Chelowski from doing something like that, Jusick had made the arrangement and the consequences clear to him by pulling a gun. As Maria tells the story, Jusick told Chelowski, "You won't do any harm to them that I won't be aware of. We will go step-by-step. We will know exactly what's going on, everything. You want the money, you want them. And I don't care if you report me. I have a way to get rid of you. Don't think that's a joke."

For his role in aiding the Devmkis, as well as other Jews and Jewish families, Jusick Gondoro-wicz and his wife were named honorary members of Yad Vashem - the musem in Israel - where a tree was planted for each of them in the "garden of Righteous Gentiles."

At some point, Jusick found Maria's brother David and brought him to the hiding place. The extra person, of course, meant extra payment. And even with all the money they had put away, after about a year, they started to run out.

David had a plan to get more money. Before the war, he had stored some clothes and suits with a woman, a widow, on a different farm. The night he went to pick up the clothes, the woman said her brother would like to buy the suits. So David sold them to him and headed back to the bunker with the money.

On the way back, he passed through a cemetery. And from behind a gravestone in that cemetery, someone stepped out - someone believed to be the woman's brother, who bought the suits -stopped David, took the money back and killed him.

This happened on a Saturday night. When Pavid didn't return on Sunday or Monday, Chelowski went into town to investigate. He came back with the news that a Jew had been killed. They didn't know for sure that it was David, but then heard that the one who was killed was wearing a checkered jacket. David had left wearing a checkered jacket. This happened in 1944, six to eight months before Maria, Fred and Rivka were liberated from their bunker.

Maria's brother, Shmuel, and his wife, Hanka (Biadak) also spent some time in the hole under the first barn floor with Maria, her husband and her mother. Fred's sister Pola Rubinek and her young boys, Alek (Alusz) and Moshe (Moniek), eight and eleven, respectively, came to hide with them there as well. But the boys did not stay long. The tiny bunker was cramped to begin with. Three extra bodies made it all but unbearable. Especially with two of them being fidgety, growing boys. The farmer was very concerned about the boys' ability to sit still and be silent for hours on end. Recall that those who protected Jews were nearly in as much danger as the Jews themselves. There were exceptions, but death was commonly the penalty for everyone involved. Those who were hidden, along with those doing the hiding.

So, on this day, recalled Chana, (then Hanka Biadak, now Chana Lewkowicz), the farmer said, "You have to leave today!" Somehow, another place was arranged for them at the home of a good friend of Chana's father. It is believed that their mutual friend and constant benefactor, Yusick Gondorowicz made the arrangements. "The evening came and Pola was afraid to go out in the fields with the kids. I said, 'Pola, look.. .you will take Moniek by the hand, and I will take Alusz, (pronounced AH-loosh),'" said Chana. "It was winter. A very strong, strong winter. And we didn't have a warm suit or coat. I took Alusz and Pola took Moniek. We came to a road that we had to cross to another road and we went like this, one, one, one, one, (single file). And then, on the way, there was a house. Big house. And suddenly, the door open and **Germans!** They saw someone was walking. They saw that we were there. The begin shooting at us. They want to kill

us! And we ran away! Everyone run away from this place. But the kids, they didn't know. Pola was with me, but the kids didn't know where we were going. (At this point, Chana chokes up at the memory.) It was a terrible time. It is still not easy for me to speak about this. - Then we came to the place, the Bozecki farm, and we stay. But without the two boys."

A day or two later, Yusick Gondorowicz came with sad news. The Germans had captured Mon-iek and taken him to the police station to kill him. "Yusick, he told us that Moniek say to them, 'Please, dont kill me here on the street. It is not far away from the cemetery where my grand-mama is. There you can kill me.'

"They took him to the cemetery. They kill him near the grave of the grandmama. And Pola, she was like.. .crazy. For her, it was a trauma. She was a beautiful, beautiful lady. Beautiful. And always she was kind. (But) all the time, 'til she passed away, it wasn't the same Pola." Pola survived the war, lived until age sixty-four in Los Angeles, and died in Kansas City, July 22, 1976.

Some time later, the son of the farmer at the place they had left - the place Fred, Maria and Rivka were hiding - was seen wearing what were believed to be Alusz' boots. They suspect Alusz tried to return to the place where Fred and Maria were hiding, but he was never heard from again.

Pola's husband, Yeshaya Leib (Shilieb) Rubinek, was also her first cousin on her father's side. Shilieb was shot and killed at a work camp. A well respected, prestigious person in the Jewish community, when told to put on the striped clothes of a slave laborer, Shilieb refused. Refused not only the change of clothes, but also refused to work in the camp. When told he would be killed for refusing, he reputedly said, "So go ahead." He was told to run, if he wanted them to kill him; that running away would give them cause. So he did. And they shot him.

Near the end, close to the time of liberation, they were all forced to leave the Chelowski farm. Not only the wife, but by then the husband wanted them to go, and said so directly. What made Mr. Chelowski want mem to leave was that in church one Sunday, he was asked point blank if he was hiding Jews on his property. The man asking the question had noticed Chelowski repairing his house using bricks. An expensive building material at the time, the man was surprised Chelowski could afford them. Chelowski explained he had collected the bricks here and there as scrap, but the suspicion alone put them all at much greater risk.

So they decided to leave the next night, heading to the town of Olszowska. They knew a farmer there by the name of Bozecki, who had done business with Maria's brother Shmuel. They did not know if he still lived there, or if he would agree to hide them. But they did know he was a poor farmer and they had some amount of money still to offer him. Maria, Fred, Rivka, Shmuel and Pola set out in the middle of the night. Dressed in farm clothes and carrying baskets, they hoped to be mistaken for farm workers, field hands.

They were stopped only once by a German who called out to them, "Where are you going?" "Home," was Maria's weary reply, returned in the German language. When he asked what they were carrying, they replied, "Eggs," which was not something the German was at all interested in. He told them all to "go to hell," but otherwise let them pass, which they all believed was a miracle sent from heaven.

The Bozeckis did take them in and hid them in the root cellar beneath the house for several months. It was there that they received the news of the liberation, that the war was over.

There was talk that the allied forces were coming, and they wanted the farmer to bring a newspaper from town. But since Bozecki himself didn't read, they were afraid it would arouse suspicion. But then Bozecki heard troops talking in Russian! That's how they knew the rumors were true.

All through that night, they heard airplanes fly past overhead. "The planes were going like 'mashugana,' (crazy). Hundreds of them," Maria recalled. They decided to risk going outside the next day. From there, they took the next step, and decided to walk back to Wodzislaw. Lacking coats, they wrapped themselves in horse blankets and set off. That was January 18, 1945.

Over the course of the war with Germany, toll on Maria's family was devastating.

Maria lost her father, Shlomo Braun, her two brothers, David Leyzer and Shmuel Yitzhak. She lost her Uncle Yosef Braun, her cousins David, Avram Shmuel, Sarah, Dina, Zalman Mendel, and Aidl, and her married cousin Shraga-Feivish, his wife Freidl and their two children, of which the eldest is known, Taube. (Freidl, Sarah, Dina and Zalman Mendel all perished at Treblinka).

Maria lost her Uncle Moshe Braun, his wife, Maria's Aunt Goldeh (Shechtman), and her cousins Tabl and Binem, who perished at Treblinka.

She lost her Uncle Noach, his wife, Maria's Aunt Rivka, and her cousins Tobeh, Binem, Brandi, and Moshe Chayim.

She lost her Aunt Sarah Gitl Braun, Aunt Sarah's husband, Noach Feuereisen and their two children, only one of whom is known, Gedalya Feuereisen.

Maria lost her paternal grandmother, Aidl (Weinreich) Braun, along with Aidl's siblings, Maria's great aunts and uncles Avraham, Pinchas, Chana and her husband, Mr. Bozekowski, Rivka and her husband, Leybish Zajac, Zelda and her husband, Mr. Fuksenhandler, and Freydeh,. Maria's Uncle David Meir Rosenberg perished, along with his step brothers Yaacov and Yehu-dis, and step sisters, Hindeh and Blumeh.

Maria's Great Aunt Miniel Rosenberg perished, along with her three children, of which two are known, Yaacov and Malka.

Her Great Uncle Yitzhak Rosenberg, his wife, Great Aunt Feltsheh and their six children, Alteh, Raizl, Heneh, Chana, Yisrael and Zeldah, all perished.

All told, Maria's father, two brothers, her Grandmother, four Aunts, six Uncles, six Great Aunts, six Great Uncles, and 22 cousins did not survive the war.

The toll on Fred's family was even greater.

Fred's mother, Kaileh (Jachimowiecz) perished. Fred's brother Shmuel Hirsh, his wife Ester Tzipeh (Mine) and their daughter, Fred's niece, Franyeh-Fradl perished at Maidanek death camp. (Fred's father, Moshe, died of an illness in 1918, when Fred was four- or five-years-old).

Fred's sister Rivka married their Uncle Shmuel Hersh Jachimowiecz. They both perished, along with three of their four children; Moshe, Gutsheh and Bibula. His brother Yankl and wife Pola (Zalcman) perished, as did their 2 children; Jadzia and Moshe. Fred's brother Fatl, his wife Bra-cha (Froman) and their infant daughter perished, as did Shileib Rubinek, Fred's sister Pola's first husband.

On Fred's father's side, his Aunt Rivka Rachel perished. Her husband, Yitzhak Goldfireund, died before the war. They had 11 children. In birth order, Shlomo, Gutsheh, Moshe, Yankle, Tova, Yisrael, Manyeh, Shmuel, David, Chaya and Sheindl.

Fred's cousin Shlomo, his wife Chava Leah (Lederman) and their two children, Ester and Manyeh, perished at Belzec. His cousin Gutsheh, her husband Motl Pszerowski and their two children, Ester Brandl and Tzirl, perished. His cousin Moshe, wife Sarah (Herszkowicz) and their three children, Leibish, Yosl and Feigl, perished. His cousin Yankl, wife Feigl (Edelist) and their two daughters, names unknown, perished. His cousin Tova and her husband Yisrael perished, as did his cousins Manyeh, David, Chaya and Sheindl. His cousin Yisrael fought as a partisan and survived the war. His cousin Shmuel survived the concentrations camps.

Fred's Aunt Zlateh, her husband Lipeh Rubinek and cousins Yeshaya Leib (Shileib), Rivka (Riftsheh), Yaacov (Yankl), Gutsheh,Yerachmiel, and Ziskind perished. Fred's Aunt Etl, her husband Tovia Lewkowicz and their daughter Gutsheh perished. His Aunt Rachl, her husband David Pinchas Goldbrom, and their six children, Nuteh, Gutsheh, Yankl, Efrayim, Chaya and Rivtsheh, all perished. His Uncle Manyeh Dziewiencki, wife Pinchas (Ko-zupske) and their two children, Moniek and Gutkeh, perished.

Fred's Great Uncle Efrayim Ha-Kohen died before the war. Five of his seven children perished; Chaya, Esther, Chana, Chayim and Yaacov.

On Fred's mother's side, besides Uncle Shmuel Hersh, who married

Fred's sister Rivka, (see above), Fred's Uncle Yaacov (Yankl), wife Chaya (Murman) and six of their eight children, Shmuel Hersh (and wife Rivka), Perl, Sheindl, Blimeh, Leah and Moshe, perished. Their eldest child, son Chayim (Hyman) survived the war, and their 5th child, daughter Gutsheh survived Leipzig-Schoenefeld, the largest concentration camp for women established by the Germans.

Fred's Uncle Moshe, wife Gitl and their six children, Avraham, Trandl, Perl, Itl, Pesl and Chayim Jachimowiecz, all perished in the Holocaust.

All told, Fred's mother, three brothers, one sister, two brothers-in-law, three sisters-in-law, five nieces, two nephews, seven Aunts, seven Uncles and 56 cousins did not survive the war.

"Yanukhim beshalom al mishkavam." - *(May they rest in peace.)*

Part 3:

From Liberation to America

1945 -1950

On what would be their final night in the make-shift hide-away in the root cellar beneath the Bedzinski family farm, Fred, Maria, Rivka and Shmuel could hear the airplanes flying overhead, one after another. "The planes were going like mashugana," Maria recalled. "Hundreds of them."

When the morning of January 18, 1945 dawned on them, they did something they had not dared to do for more than two years. They went outside in broad daylight.

They had heard rumors that allied forces, liberation from Germany and the end of the war were all close at hand. While a simple newspaper might have confirmed this, they feared it would arouse suspicion if the benevolent, but illiterate farmer was seen in town trying to buy one. But then, the farmer himself became a news reporter when he saw new troops and heard them speaking Russian. The allies had finally arrived!

Wrapped in horse blankets to ward off the cold, Fred, Maria, Rivka and Shmuel, set off walking to Wodzislaw. When they got there, the first person they saw was someone they knew. A Jewish man who confirmed the good news. "The Russians are here," he told them. "Don't worry."

Moving through town, they went first to the house of Esther Jevinsky, wife of Chiam. It was empty. They went on to the home where Maria and her mother had lived, only to find it occupied by the Polish Postmeister. The German occupiers had given him their home. Rebuffed, they returned to Esther Jevinsky's house to spend the night.

Maria and her mother, Rivka, returned to their former home the next day and confronted the man living there, telling him that they rightfully owned the property. He replied that no one owned that house anymore and threatened them, telling them to leave. Rivka persisted, saying she wanted no trouble, but asking could she go inside to gather some family pictures? The man agreed. A portrait they found in the attic that day still hangs in Maria's Kansas City home.

Maria went to the home of the burgomeister's sister-in-law, her childhood school friend and witness at her wedding. Maria had left clothing and other items with her before they fled into hiding. When the door opened Maria was greeted with disbelief; contemptuous disbelief. "You're still alive!?!"

In disbelief herself, Maria said, "'I really don't want more than my clothes.' And I left a lot with her. And she said, 'I'm very sorry. I have nothing. The German organization' - whatever it was -'took everything out and I have nothing of yours. - I'm sorry. You have to leave.'

"I said, 'Oh, it's a very nice greeting you give me after all the friendship we had for all that time!' She took out two potatoes and tried to give them to me. She said, 'I give this to you and you will have a dinner.'

"I threw them on the floor and walked out. - I never saw her again," said Maria.

Not long after that, Maria and Fred decided there was no life for them in Wodzislaw. They made plans to move to the larger city of Sosnowiec 74 km, about 46 miles, away. Maria's mother, Rivka, decided to stay in Wodzislaw and try to find a way to legally get her house back, which, much to her credit, she eventually did. Maria's brother, Shmuel stayed with Rivka in Wodzislaw.

Once in Sosnowiec, Maria went to the courthouse to see if there were any Brauns living there or if there was property the family might have owned. She found that her uncle, Moshe Braun, owned a furniture factory. He also owned a large house with a storefront right on Main Street. Uncle Moshe gave them the Main Street property. They lived in the house and turned the storefront into a grocery.

Maria contacted farmers she knew from before the war, and other farmers in smaller surrounding communities, and had them bring their goods - flour, eggs, chickens and produce - to Sosnowiec. She would buy from the farmers and sell to the people in the city.

Around September, 1945, after they had been in business for 6 or 7 months, Yusick Gondoro-wicz helped them again. Yusick found an old truck that he gave to Shmuel in Wodzislaw and put him in the business, showing him the routes to the farmers. Shmuel would then go to the farmers, collect their goods and drive the loaded truck to Sosnowiec. Then, on the return trips, he would load up the truck with washing machines, sewing machines, bicycles and other goods from Sosnowiec. "Things that the little cities didn't have," said Maria, to sell to farmers and merchants in the smaller towns. Actually, most of these goods were exchanged, or bartered, rather than "bought and sold" in the traditional sense. "Cause nobody had money," said Maria. "It was an exchange. So, that creates a business. I created a food store. A grocery."

The grocery business was doing well. So well, that they had to hire a woman to help them work the store. So well, that Maria wanted to bring Shmuel and Rivka to join them in Sosnowiec.

"One good day," said Maria, "I find a place for Shmuel from another uncle, a house, and I said, 'It's time for you to leave Wodzislaw. You don't have nobody there and nobody from the family is coming back. Move. Bring my mother. Here's a place. And I can get this in three weeks. I can get the papers worked out and you can get the house. That night, he went with me, we made arrangements. I showed him the house and he liked it. So, he put a load of bicycles in his truck and he went back home to pick up my mother and his girlfriend. He said he's going home to sell the bicycles and take care of whatever, financial, and a month or so he would move to Sosnowiec." That was the last time Fred & Maria would ever see him. That night, May 1, 1945, Shmuel was killed.

He had returned late to Wodzislaw, about 11:15 pm, with the truckload of bicycles. He parked the truck in a safe place - where they lived was not a safe place to leave a truck full of goods -and started walking home. He arrived about midnight. As soon as he entered the house, two men came to the door. When Rivka answered, they burst in, chased Shmuel through the house and shot him dead in a room at the back as he tried to escape through a window.

The two men were members of the Polish Army of Kriova, the AK; (the "ah-kah," Maria said). The AK was anti-German when Germany occupied Poland and now they were anti-Russian, because the Russians occupied their country. In a deadly case of mistaken identity, the men mistook Shmuel for another man who lived in the same building. It was this other man who was working with the Russians. Shmuel was buried by the AK in the Wodzislaw cemetery next to a mass grave.

Since the phone lines were not working between Wodzislaw and Sosnowiec at that time, it was a day or two later that Yusik Gondorowicz drove the 74 kilometers to Sosnowiec with the news.

"He came into my store. We sit and talk. He said, 'I have bad news for you." I said, 'What, again? A new war?' You know, what else could I think? I already lost what I had to lose. My father's gone. My other brother's gone. I said, 'My momma's sick?'

"He said, 'No. They killed your brother.'

"I said, 'What? What are you saying?' -1 didn't even believe it. I thought he was trying to joke with me. I said, 'Mr. Gondorowicz, what are you talking about?'

"He said, 'They killed your brother. He got home 11:15 in the truck. Twelve o'clock they killed him. He's dead. Can't you understand?' And, he said, 'I have more news for you. You'd better leave. Both of you. You and your husband.' He said, 'They're afraid that you will find out who killed your brother. They said they have to go after Fred, because, otherwise they're in danger.'"

Gondorowicz himself was a member of the AK, but had his own personal loyalties, too. He had been at a meeting where the men who killed Shmuel said they planned to go after Fred, for they feared he would discover what had happened and come looking for them, seeking revenge. Not so much physically, as legally. The men feared that when a true legal system re-emerged, they could be prosecuted for Shmuel's murder. So, they planned to come for Fred first.

Seeking a way out, Fred and Maria got a car and drove to Krakow to meet a Mr. Knobler, her father's attorney from before the war. She explained the situation and said, "I want to get away from all of it, as soon as I can."

As Maria recalled it, he said, "You know it's not so easy.'

"I said, 'How much do we need for that?'

"He said, 'It's not just money. It'll take time.'

"I said, 'No. It will take 24 hours, and you will do it!'

Maria gave him the money they had. Over nine months in the grocery business, they had made about $4,000. Knobler told them to stay in Krakow with him and his wife and he would see what he could do.

The very next day, a Russian truck with a Russian guide came for them. Knobler said the Russian would take them to the border of Czechoslovakia, but not across, because he promised the Russian he would not have to endanger his own life. Knobler told them every road across the border was guarded by armed soldiers at checkpoint stations, but he also told them not to worry,

said Maria, because, "You're not going to go through the roads. You are going through the forest." And he gave them a map with a path to follow safely across the border.

The Russian dropped them off late that night near the Czech border.

"The forest was pitch dark," said Maria. "It's maybe 11:00-12:00 o'clock at night. What do you see in a forest? Trees! How do you know where to go? - It was late. We was so tired. So exhausted." So, instead of trying to feel their way through the dark woods, they found a place to rest for the night.

At first light, they began their walk, following the map Knobler had given them. The map eventually led them out of the forest to the edge of Prague, Czechoslovakia's largest city. At the edge of the woods, they met two other men from Krakow trying to get away from Poland, and the four of them decided to go into town together. Without a penny to their names, they walked into a restaurant and hoped for the best.

"We sit down. We ask for cup of warm water, 'cause we know we have no money to pay," said Maria.

A local gentleman seated nearby noticed that they did not speak Czech. He tried German. "Sprechen sie deutsch?" Which they did. Maria asked the man if he could help them; "Konnen sie mir helfen?" And that they needed a bit of sustenance. "We need a cup of tea or a cup of coffee, or something," said Maria. "He said, 'All four. I get all that..., and breakfast.'

"Not just coffee, we had breakfast! And he sits, and he waits. And when we finish he said, 'You need a bath.' I said, 'I know, we were in the forest all night long!'

"He took us all home. He said, 'Here is a shower. Here is a bedroom. Help yourself.' He even gave the men shirts. For me, he didn't have anything. So, I wash my things and hang them in the bathroom to dry out. He said, 'By the time I come back, I find out how you can go farther from here.' - And he went off to work."

At 4:00 o'clock that afternoon, the man returned and took them all to another cafe for dinner. "I remember," said Maria, "it was just potato soup. Everybody got a little potato soup." But more than that, the man took them all to the train station, put them on a train and paid for their tickets. Telling them to get off wherever they liked. They took that train to a city somewhere in Austria.

When they got off the train, they found an organization set up to help Jewish refugees. That group directed them to the gemeinde, the city hall, that had barracks with a few hundred beds where they could sleep. But on the way there, a miracle happened. There, on the street, they ran into familiar faces. Some people Fred had done textile business with before the war. When these friends heard where they were going to spend the night, Maria recalled, "They said, 'You're not going no place. It's the High Holidays! We all staying here.'"

When the holidays were over, it was time to move on. A Jewish organization funded by support from America, and other countries, provided them food, clothing and a little money. They boarded a train heading out of Austria and into Germany. When the train stopped at Regensberg, they all got off and went to look for the local gemeinde. Once there, they were asked if they wanted to go on to Munich, where the main gemeinde for all of Germany was located, with the potential to provide the most help. Especially for immigration. But no, they decided to stay in Regensberg.

After staying that very first night at the Regensberg gemeinde, another miraculous thing happened. The very next day, said Maria, "everyone got a place to live! A single man moved in with a family. A couple got a little house or two rooms. It seems impossible. It was possible!"

While it may be counterintuitive that they would choose to live in Germany, it was the place they felt would provide them the best opportunity to prepare for their next move. "The papers were saying, in every German newspaper, that councils were working on paperwork to send the children to Israel or America," said Maria. Neither Austria nor Czechoslovakia had the level of organizational structure that was set up in Germany at that time.

While there, an American soldier came to visit them and asked if he could be of any assistance. Maria told him about her mother back home in Wodzislaw and that she wanted to go there and find her. The soldier arranged some sort of transit pass for Maria and with it, she hitchhiked back to Wodzislaw, found her mother, packed her up, and brought her to Regensberg.

With the remnants of their family reunited, Fred, Maria and Rivka tried to find work there. On one street, Maria had noticed a milliners shop for ladies' hats that looked to be a good store, in a good location, but there was never anybody there running the place. So she went to city hall to inquire about the shop. She was told that no one knew when, or if, the owners would return, or if they were even alive. But city officials gave her a date and said that if the owners had not returned by then, they would talk to Maria and Fred about taking the store over.

In the meantime, Maria got a job working for the burgomeister, the mayor, of Regensberg. It was the burgomeister who gave final approval for Fred and Maria to run the milliners shop, paying rent to the Mayor for the space. They ran that shop for three years, before coming to America.

In a 1994 interview, Maria talked about the government payment system in Regensberg at that time. "We have to have some little stamps to buy clothes, to buy food, to buy anything like that. "Now the poor people get food stamps. Then, it was even rich people. We have no choice. There

was not too much to buy for money, but for stamps. You have a need for a dress, they give you so many stamps. If you have need for socks, for hose, whatever, that's what the business was."

What they had been told that first night in the Regensberg gemeinde was true. The main gemeinde for immigration was in Munich. Maria went there to apply to a Jewish agency dealing with hopeful immigrants.

"They say, 'If you register, you can go to United States.' I say, 'Where is that?' " said Maria. "They say, 'You know, America, United States!"

"I didn't know about America, but I say wherever we going to be, let it be away from Poland. I don't want Poland. I'm not going back." Maria wanted to go to a place, "where they don't know us; they don't know anything of us. The only thing I didn't like about America, because my

mother always told me stories, they sell people on the street." Rivka had told her children the tale of slavery in America. She had one other sad American tale to tell.

When the first World War broke out, Rivka had been engaged to a young man from a wealthy family in they city of Lodg, Poland. The marriage never happened, because her fiancee's father shipped Rivka's fiancee off to America to avoid serving in the Polish army.

It was 1947 in Regensberg that Rivka, Fred, Maria and the newest member of the family, initially registered for immigration. In the order of things, young people were given top priority, then older unmarried people, then families with children. Fred and Maria fell into the final category with the arrival of their new son, Solomon Moses "Sam" Devinki, born in Regensberg, June 9, 1946.

While Maria maintained that she didn't know anything about America, there was someone in America who knew about them. Fred had an uncle living in Brooklyn, New York. They had corresponded, hoping the uncle could provide "sponsorship" for them. A "sponsor" in this sense, was someone willing and able to offer an immigrant work upon arrival. Such a sponsorship would speed up the immigration process.

"We would like for somebody to sponsor us," said Maria. "We don't need any support. We're young. We can work. We can do anything possible, just...the sooner is better."

Unfortuantely, Fred's uncle "was an older gentlemen," said Maria, "and he was retired. Of course he was trying, (but), if you don't have a business, you can't really sponsor too many people. We were three people to sponsor."

Three years would pass before they finally had the chance to leave Germany for a new life.

"It was '47 when I register. In '50 I got the Visa. The visa was for Kansas City. You know, I went to the library. I want to see where Kansas City is," said Maria. "I didn't like it. You know why? On the map, it was shown as hilly. And it's a country city. Lot of farmers. Lot of cows and horses and cowboys. And I said, 'Oh no. I'm not going there. What else you have?'

"They said, "That's the visa. When you get there, you can do as you please. Right now, you have to go according to the visa.'" And so they did. In early February, 1950, Fred, Maria, Rivka and young Sam boarded the government transport ship "USS General McRae" with 2,000 fellow passengers bound for New York harbor.

Young Solomon Moses Devinki's earliest memories were formed on that ship. "I would have been about 4 years old and recollections from that age are more like a dream than they are real," said Sam, "but here's what I remember. I got sick on the ship. I don't remember exactly what I had, but I had something that was contagious. Some kind of childhood disease that was contagious,

(Sam had the measles). Whatever this area was that I was being quarantined in, I was in a medical area.

"I remember a baby crib that had a mesh thing over the top to keep me from climbing out. I actually remember my grandmother sleeping underneath this crib with me at night, because I was afraid. I also remember climbing out of this bed. The net was diamond shaped, so there were little corners. And I climbed out through one of these corners. I remember taking a couple of little things with me, like kids would have, a blanket or a doll, whatever, but I had something, and I remember climbing up a set of metal stairs to a door. And that's all I remember. That is my total recollection. - So I guess I was caught at the door."

The voyage was to take 18 days. But after about 15 days at sea, the ship struck an iceberg and began slowly taking on water. Unable to repair it, a second ship was dispatched from New York, and within a day the passengers were transferred to the second ship, the USS General W.M. Black, the "General Schwartz," as Maria called it. The passengers changed sips as they floated side-by-side, in mid-ocean.

With that slight, and slightly harrowing, delay, they steamed on into New York harbor. But that was not their final destination. Fred, Maria and Sam were supposed to go first to New Orleans and then on to Kansas City from there. But for some reason, there was a discrepancy with the passport of Maria's mother. Apparently Rivka was slated to disembark in New York. Fortunately, Maria was able to convince the New York authorities that Rivka would be left there all alone and that, as her daughter, she would gladly sign for her mother, so that Rivka could continue on with the family.

They stayed in New York harbor for 24 hours while the ship took on fresh provisions, and the next day they sailed off to New Orleans. That trip took three more days.

When they arrived in New Orleans, nurses there wanted to take little Sam to a quarantine area that was different from where the others were told to go. They needed to be sure, said Maria, "that he's safe. That he's not in danger or that somebody's not going to catch the disease from him, or whatever." Their initial intent was to take Sam away to quartantine without his mother. Maria had other intentions. "I said, 'I'm going where my child goes!' And we had a big fight with the nurses. There was a bunch of nurses. And they let me get in that little..., that little car with the 'wa-woo-woo-woo-woo-woo!' (an ambulance)."

It was not only about the measles, they were afraid Sam might also have strep throat and would still be contagious and a danger to others. So Sam was taken to an area hospital for observation. After appropriate tests were run, he was cleared and released the very next day.

The next three days were spent getting their identification, transfer and transportation papers in order with the help of a Jewish organization in New Orleans. "And then," said Maria, "they put us on a train and sent us to Kansas City."

Part 4

A New Beginning

1950 to Here and Now

Once the train pulled into Kansas City's Union Station, Fred, Maria, Sam and Grandma Rivka found help at the local Jewish aid organization, the Benjamin Clinic. Today, that same organization is operating as Jewish Family and Children Services, under the umbrella of the Jewish Federation. Through the Benjamin Clinic, they found a place to live, which Sam recollects as 710 Virginia. (As an aside, all of the Devinki children, Sam, Karen and Ida, have encyclopedic memories for property addresses.) With a roof over their heads, Fred and Maria set their minds to the problem of how to pay for it.

Back at the aid organization, trying to find work, they asked Fred what he did? Fred asked them, "What do you need?" They said, "We need a painter." Fred said, "I'm a painter!" So they got him a job as a painter.

That job ended in a disagreement over duties. One day the job foreman, who has been described as a "rotten S.O.B.," wanted Fred to paint the capstone of the chimney at Twin Oaks apartments, at 50th and Oak. Twin Oaks was a 20-story building. The capstone rose 2-stories above the roof; the building's highest and most dangerous point. The disagreement was over whether to go with the foreman's plan to paint the capstone, or Fred's suggestion to take that job and "stuff it!" Fred won the disagreement... and the chance to look for a new job.

Drawing on their extensive retail experience, Fred and Maria went into partnership with a Sam Ruizga (spelling uncertain), to open their first Kansas City business, a fruit stand at 31st and Garfield. It was not the best, nor safest location in town.

Sam Devinki tells the family story of the time Maria thwarted a robbery there. A man came in at closing time, pulled a gun and demanded that Maria put all the money from the cash drawer into a bag. Maria, cooly and calmly, pulled out the day's receipts and started counting. The man was incredulous. "What are you doing!?!"

"I'm counting the money," Maria said. "I have to know how much you're taking." Never expecting an answer like that, the man ultimately panicked and ran off- empty handed.

Although uncertain of exactly when that happened, "the story ran in the Kansas City Star," sometime in the early '50s, said Sam, when Maria would have been in her early 30s.

But it wasn't the dicey location that ultimately broke up that business partnership. It was the partner. Son Sam recalls hearing that Sam Ruizga was a tough guy, a macho guy, with a hot temper and that he and Fred had trouble getting along.

"They were both hot-headed," Sam Devinki said. The partnership didn't last, but the business did. Fred and Maria re-opened the store in 1952, at the corner of 27th Street and Van Brunt Boulevard. The "Volume Dollar Mkt.," 2701 Van Brunt, was so small, (or the sign so big), they had to use the abbreviated form of "Market" to get their name out there, selling groceries of all sorts along with meat, fruit and fresh produce.

The window sign promised "CUT RATE PRICES." Specifically advertised were "Eggs for .85 cents," "Lean meat spare ribs .39 cents lb," "Chuck roast .29 cents lb," and "Chili 3 lbs for $1.00."

It was later that same year, 1952, that Fred and Maria made their first venture into real estate; buying a home for the family at 4439 Tracy.

"I think that was the first real house that we had," Sam recalled. "I was 6 or 7 by then. I had my own bedroom there, which was kind of an attic area, a finished attic area which was kind of neat. And I remember having a cat in that house."

He also remembers his grandmother, Rivka Braun, who had emigrated with them from Germany, buying the house next door at 4441 Tracy.

"She was an exceptionally wonderful woman. She's the one that actually raised me, because my mother was working. She raised me. She raised Karen. She didn't have much chance to raise Ida, because she died when Ida was 3 or 4. She was an incredibly wonderful woman. And my grandmother, as well as my parents, were dedicated to their children.

"My grandmother was a business woman. That's where my mother got it from. My grandmother understood business and she, in her own little way, did some real estate stuff. This was a woman who had no education in this country, barely could speak English, but yet, had the wherewithal to run a rental property; to fix it up, to lease it out, to do whatever needed to be done. For a single woman, she had remarkable skills. And you have to remember, her husband was taken to Treblinka and murdered in 1941. She did everything on her own and from what I understand now, she was probably responsible for the fact that my mother and father survived, *and* came to this country.

Rivka's "chutzpah" was legendary. To follow a story told briefly the previous chapter, in 1945, at the end of the war, Rivka went back to Wozislaw, to the house they had lived in before the war, only to find a Polish postal official living there. The man had been given the house by the Germans. "No," Rivka said. "This isn't your house. This is my house." Rivka convinced the man that she wanted no trouble and was able to gather some personal belongings from the house before she left. - She left, but eventually returned. This time with the law on her side.

"She actually filed a lawsuit," said Sam. "She went to court in the equivalent of their county seat, which was a town called Yengiev, about 10 miles away from Wodzislaw. They had a hearing and she brought proof that it was her house. She proved it and the presiding judge issued an order, which I have, saying, This house belongs to Regina Braun.' This is a woman, in 1945, who did this on her own. No husband. No lawyer. She did this on her own," Sam marveled. - He marveled all the more, as he fondly recalled the story of his grandmother and his first new bike.

"My parents called from the Western Auto Store at 31st and Troost and they wanted my grandmother to bring me down there. They were going to buy me a bicycle for my birthday. It was a 3-speed English racer. And I was sooo excited! I ran all the way from the house to the trolley stop at 45th and Troost!

"Of course, my poor grandmother couldn't keep up with me. The trolley came and my grandmother was still half a block back, so I was going to try and catch the trolley and hold it.

"Well, I got my foot in the door, but the driver didn't see me. He closed the door and the trolley started moving, and my foot was caught in the door! It was literally a miracle that I got my foot out of my shoe. I was pretty upset and crying, because I'd almost been killed.

"My grandmother finally got there, and this nice man, who I guess was following the trolley and had seen the whole thing, took me and my grandmother and we chased the trolley down and he actually recovered my shoe from the trolley and scolded the driver. It was quite a traumatic thing. But to me, once I got past the initial shock, it was no big deal, because I was getting a 3-speed bike! That was all that was important."

At about this same time, sometime in 1954, Fred and Maria were forced to move out of their small grocery store at 27th and Van Brunt. "They had a two-year lease," said Sam, "and they didn't understand about leases. When the lease was up the guy who owned it wouldn't renew because he said Deluxe Cleaners was interested in the spot and they were going to pay a lot more rent. "Well, all their assets were tied up in the fixtures, because that's all a grocery store is. If you don't have a location, what do you do? So, they moved down to 4th and Walnut and opened a fruit market there."

Fred and Maria had acquired quite a nest egg from their entrepreneurial efforts back in Regensberg. Sam believes they brought about $40,000 dollars with them when they came over from Germany. In 1950, $40,000 was a considerable sum, but somewhat less than they thought.

"They figured they had enough money to last them for 40 years," said Sam. "They figured whatever money they made here, if they supplemented that with this $40,000, they could live for the next 40 years and everything would be great. The problem is, by the time they got kicked out of this grocery store, that whole $40,000 was gone. And we're talking a period of about two to three years!"

As fate would have it, however, it was also in 1954 that Fred and Maria Devinki's destiny would take a lasting turn toward prosperity. While still working the store, Maria thought, "I'm not going to stay at the cash register. That's not what I want to do. I want to do something else. So I start looking for...what kind of business is in this world? I'm not in Germany any more. What do they have in this country that is good? Where you can make a living without being a slave. So, I see in the paper a lot of ads, in the Sunday paper, for real estate, real estate, real estate. Every page was real estate. I didn't know what that means, because it didn't mean anything in my language."

Mind you, Maria knew several languages. She was raised speaking Yiddish and Polish. She spoke German, some Russian and a little Czech. So English was not a second language, but a fourth or fifth. And it was in the Sunday newspaper that Maria found her first "fortune" in another language she spoke very well.

Maria's eldest daughter, Karen Pack, explains: "Had the war not happened, my mother would have been a math teacher. She's a numbers person. And real estate was a very numbers oriented business. You can buy it for this number, rent it for that number, then fix it up and sell it for another number. It's not so much that you need the language skills, it's all about the numbers.

"And as my father once said, 'You know, when I was in the grocery store business I sold apples. I made apple sauce. In the real estate business I sold apartments. I made money! Selling one apartment makes a lot more money than selling 100 apples!'"

The piece of real estate that caught Maria's eye in the Sunday paper that fateful day was a 3-story house at 31st and Broadway. "I said to Fred, 'Now wait a minute. We can make three apartments from this.' He said, 'How would they have a kitchen?' I said, 'We make the first floor an apartment. Second floor, we bring up the plumbing from the first floor.'"

But, first things first. First they had to buy the property. That next day, on Monday, Maria went to talk to the real estate agent. The house was priced at $7,000.

"Well, first of all," Sam Devinki recalled, "the house was $7,000 dollars. They didn't have 7,000 pennies. So she borrowed $2,000 from her cousin in New Jersey, Al Braun."

For the remaining $5,000, they went for a loan where their business account was held, across the street to Merchant's Produce Bank, on the corner of 4th and Walnut. Sam Schultz was the owner of that bank, and that's who Maria went to talk to.

"I need to borrow $5,000," said Maria. "I want to buy this house. I have $2,000 and I want to borrow $5,000." Naturally, Sam Schultz asked, 'Well, what's your collateral?"

As Maria tells the story, "I said, 'What's collateral?'" It was an English word that was a foreign concept to her. "He said, 'Something to put under.' I said, 'To put under what?' I didn't understand what he was trying to tell me."

Fortunately, Sam Schultz spoke Yiddish, as did Maria. In Yiddish, he explained that collateral was something a borrower needed to have to guarantee, or secure, a loan.

"He said, 'You have to have you have some resources put aside; other houses or bonds or stock, or whatever.' And in Yiddish, I say to him, 'No. I don't have any of that. I don't have anything.' But I opened my coat, I said, 'Here! You see me? *That's* your collateral!'

"He said, 'You are good collateral,'" and he loaned her the $5,000 dollars.

At that time, the 28 or 29-year-old Maria didn't have much of anything in terms of material wealth. But what she did have would server her so much better. What she had was summed up by one of the architects Fred and Maria worked with over the years, recorded in the video honoring the 50th anniversary of Devinki Real Estate.

"She had that keen eye," said James Taylor, Principal architect at James E. Taylor and Associates. "Seeing some property, recognizing what it could be in future, how much she should pay for it, how much she would have to invest in it, and what would be her return on it. She just had that keen eye. As well as a very intelligent mind that would allow her to pursue that. And she had the trust of many people."

The trust of Sam Shultz proved to be a very good start. Maria and Fred took the loan and bought the house intending to fix it up and rent it out as a 3-plex apartment. Fate had other ideas.

The property stood very near the offices of Kansas City Life Insurance company. A company that was expanding, growing, gaining employees. Employees with cars who needed a place to park them. In a classic case of being in the ri^it place at the right time, Fred and Maria Devinki now owned the right place to put up that parking lot. And Kansas City Life wanted to pay them handsomely for it. Still, it was not the easiest business transaction to complete.

"I had a telephone call from Kansas City Life," Maria said. "I thought they want me to buy some life insurance. I hung up."

As Sam Devinki tells it, "She hangs up on him, because she thinks something is not kosher, not legal. There's something funny about this. People don't just call you up and say, 'I want to buy your house.' So, a day or two later, this guy, I think his name was Paul Murphy, a Vice President at Kansas City Life, but I'm not sure. Anyway, whoever the guy was, he shows up down at the fruit stand, all dressed up in his suit, and says, 'Hello Mrs. Devinki, I spoke to you on the phone the other day. You have a piece of property on Broadway next to Kansas City Life.'

"She says, 'Yes, I do. Anything wrong?'

"He says, 'No, but Kansas City Life would like to buy it from you.'

"She says, 'It's not for sale.'

"He says, 'I don't think you understand. We don't need your property. We need your land. We're going to buy that whole block. We're going to tear it down. We're going build a parking lot for Kansas City Life.'

"He says, 'We know you paid $7,000 dollars. We'll pay you $14,000.' So this is a $7,000 profit in less than a year - and in 1954, that's big money. Then he says, 'I'll help you even more. We won't close the deal until after you've owned it for a full year, so that you get your capital gains. We'll also help you find another piece of property.'"

Good as his word, KC Life paid them $14,000, doubling their initial investment, along with doubling their number of real estate transactions - from one to two - in under a year. This was followed closely by their third transaction, just down the street at Armour and Central. The $7,000 profit made the perfect down payment on "The Colonies;" a complex of six, 4-plex apartment buildings.

Within a year of purchasing The Colonies, history repeated itself. Those six 4-plex apartments happened to stand where Union Life insurance company wanted to build their new national headquarters. Union Life bought the whole block from Fred and Maria. Devinki Real Estate was born.

"That's how it got started. It was those two deals," said Sam, "which were both due to this guy at Kansas City Life. All of which came about because they were kicked out of that grocery store."

In 1956, the family moved to 1008 W. 70th Terrace and operated Devinki Real Estate from that home for more than a decade. By 1959, Devinki Real Estate was a true success story. They had acquired more than 10 buildings. Fred did the repairs. Maria painted and purchased second hand items to furnish the apartments.

Among the properties purchased in 1959 was "The Ricardo," a run down hotel and apartment building at 811 E. Armour. Occupancy at The Ricardo wasn't bringing in enough revenue to cover expenses, but that was not the bank's problem. They still wanted the mortgage loan to be paid on time and were threatening to foreclose.

Fred and Maria were at a loss for what to do to make the necessary payments, when Maria once again found a story in the Kansas City Star that saved the day. The story told about the Housing and Urban Development Department, HUD, offering what were known as 221 D3 loans administered through the Federal Housing Administration, FHA, to developers willing to convert older buildings into housing for the elderly.

Maria believed The Ricardo would be a perfect candidate for the program. So she got on a plane and flew to Washington, D.C. to present her case. The FHA agreed. Maria got the money - a 30-year loan of $600,000 at 3% interest. The Ricardo became known as the Homestead. It was the largest construction project ever undertaken by Devinki Real Estate. According to Sam, it's a testament to their stability, to their intention to be in it for the long haul, that Devinki Real Estate was the only company in Kansas City that originated a 221 D3 loan and kept the property for the full 30 years, until the loan was paid off.

Maria Devinki became known around town and further afield, as a person with a keen eye and good sense for real estate. A newspaper article around this time noted that only two Kansas City real estate companies had managed to avoid property foreclosures; Devinki Real Estate and J.C. Nichols.

"They compared me to J.C. Nichols," said Maria with a laugh, and gave a comparison of her own. "I was a penny. He was a dollar!"

What she may have lacked in quantity, she made up for in quality. Maria understood the subtleties of how much a given property was worth. Not how much it was selling for, but what it was worth. The ability to realistically estimate how much it would take to renovate a property and what the ultimate return on that investment might be. She also had a very good sense of what time was the right time to sell it.

"Eveiything has a limit," said Maria. "I'd rather have it in my pocket than in the bush. When I see the profit is enough, maybe it's going to be higher next year, two years from now, but right now, I'm selling it."

Much more importantly for Maria, she also became known as a woman of her word.

"When you had a conversation with (Fred and Maria) and they stated what they were going to do, they did it," said architect, James Taylor.

"If I said something, I wouldn't change," said Maria. "If I said something, it was delivered. There couldn't be any changes, even if I be a loser, that's the way it is. I wouldn't change."

Escrow Officer, Dorothy Dismang, recalled her first dealings with Maria. "My boss, when he was first describing her to me, in the first closing I was going to have, he told me, 'You will find this lady so honest, that if she tells you the sun's going to come up in the west tomorrow morning, just go out on the west side of your house and wait for it. It will be there.' -I learned from Maria the most important thing you can do in life is to always keep your word."

With her word as her bond, Maria said, "I sold every piece of property on a hand shake."

A very memorable hand shake happened in 1977. Maria and Fred Devinki, their son Sam and real estate agent Joe Burgland were meeting in the office of attorney, Phil Kurwin to seal a deal worth over $2 million for the purchase of Plaza Point, 4901 Wornall Road in Kansas City, the current headquarters of Devinki Real Estate. An agreement was reached, Maria and Mr. Kurwin shook hands and were preparing to sign the requisite paperwork when there was a knock at the door. It was Mr. Kurwin's partner, saying there was an urgent matter they needed to discuss immediately. Mr. Kurwin excused himself and stepped into the hall. The urgent matter was a better offer from another potential buyer. And, after all, the papers had not yet been properly, legally signed.

"We have an offer $100,000 more than your offer," said Mr. Kurwin, when he returned to the room, "but it's too late. I shook hands with you. I will not back out.'

'Tomorrow morning, 10 o'clock," said Maria, "I'll be here with a check."

"I trust you," said Mr. Kurwin. And that was that. That $2 million dollar property was sold and closed without a written contract, on the strength of Maria Devinki's handshake.

Yet, even with the sealed deal firmly in hand, there would still be written contracts that needed to be clearly understood and legally acted upon. Contracts written in English. While Maria's reputation for honesty was unshakeable, her eye for real estate undeniable, and her understanding of facts and figures unquestionable, her grasp of written property contracts was sometimes tenuous at best. As mentioned earlier, English was not a second language to Fred and Maria, it was more like their fourth or fifth. So the responsibility of reading important contracts often fell to their young son, Sam.

"There were so many languages they spoke," said daughter Karen. "And by the time they got to English, can you imagine how hard it must have been? My mother was 30 when she came here. My father was in his late 30s. My grandmother was in her 50s. And there was no 'spell check.' So, Sam was doing all that; read this contract, do this, do that. So, he had a lot placed on him. And he still does."

Sam's sister, Karen Erleen Devinki, came along as a beautiful little tax deduction, on April 15th, 1951. To make room for the darling new addition, the family moved to 4439 Tracy, in the house right across the driveway from their grandmother, Rivka. Karen and Rivka were very close in more ways than one.

"My grandmother was pretty much in charge of the day-to-day taking care of me," Karen recalled. "My parents were working. My mother was a career woman before it was fashionable.

"(Rivka) had a wonderful porch with a screen in the front. She had a swing in the back yard. And I feel I am the person today, the mother I am today, because of how she took care of me. She was wonderful. We made sandwiches together. We went on picnics together. Went to the park together. We went shopping at the 'goodwill' together. You know, when you're a little kid and you don't have any money, it's great!

"My grandmother could sew. Take a scrap of anything and make a ball gown out of it. So she always made clothes for my dolls. And my grandmother could *fix* anything from shoes to clothes to jewelry to furniture. Anything. She had, like, a whole little workshop in the back of her house. So whatever I needed, she just always made it happen.

"She always had wonderful meals. She made fabulous chicken soup. And to make the soup go longer, she would break in matza instead of noodles. I don't know if we had noodles, but matza is cheaper. It was wonderful, too. All these things that now you think were inexpensive, then they were all a treat.

"She made her own buttermilk! She made fabulous buttermilk. Cold buttermilk and boiled potatoes. They were incredible. And she made the most incredible apple sauce. Her applesauce was so great, I can't eat jarred apple sauce. It just tastes awful. And I can't drink (commercial) buttermilk, because it doesn't compare to her buttermilk. I so wish I would have gotten those recipes, because I've never been able to replicate them."

In 1956, when the family moved to West 70th Terrace, they looked for a house nearby for Rivka, but it took a year to find one. "And that was really a lonely year," said Karen. "I was already in school by then, 1st grade. I finished Kindergarten at Bancroft and started 1st grade at Hale Cook. Tough Principal, there. Mrs. Daw.

"Sam is five years older. So, when I was at Hale Cook in 1st grade, he was in the 6th grade. Well, he was a big cool guy. And I was a little runt, you know? This big cool guy isn't going to hang out with his sister. That just wasn't cool. Even though we'd walk home together, he'd walk, you know, ahead of me, down the street. There was enough of an age difference that we lived in the same house, but had very different lives.

"We lived in a primarily Catholic neighborhood. It was St. Elizabeth's parish. Most of the kids went to St. Elizabeth's. Those were the days where, since most mothers were home, everyone kept an eye out for everybody else's kid. Anyone saw you needed something,....they were there. And if you did the wrong thing, somebody's mother was there to pull you up by the hair.

"I had the greatest childhood in the world. I never felt that my life wasn't that of a princess, (accent on the second syllable!) My mother could also sew and crochet and things like that. I had, in my opinion, the most beautiful clothes, that my mother would make. Like the party dress for my birthday. She decked me out."

There were many times when Karen was decked out, Sam recalls the time she was knocked out.

"I was carrying Karen on the handle bars of my bicycle and I made a turn and, of course, with her weight, it got the bike off balance and we fell," said Sam. "She hit her head. She was knocked out. She was out cold. I thought I killed her. We took her home and everything was pretty traumatic. She actually had a concussion."

Sam also remembered an early effort at running his own business. "While we lived at 1008 W. 70th Terrace, we used to have these big snowfalls," said Sam. "Of course, I was always interested in making money, and I realized you could make money by shoveling snow. Except it was really hard work! So I got Billy Shifinan, and a couple other younger kids in the neighborhood, and I would go procure the jobs and they would shovel, and we would split the money. I figured that was a better deal than doing the shoveling!"

In the Devinki family, business was how you survived. It was how you took care of your family. It was how you made sure there was enough for education. It was how you made sure there was enough to help somebody in need, whether it was a family member or a stranger.

"My parents worked full time," said Karen. "They had gone through a time when they'd lost *everything*. They had less than nothing. So, it was an act of survival. My parents didn't play golf. They didn't play cards. They didn't run around town. They worked.

"My father worked very, very long hours. He worked very hard. My mother worked every day, except when it came to a Jewish Holiday.

"At that time in their lives, there wasn't time off for vacationing. There wasn't extra time to go have fun as people look at it today. But when it came to a Holiday, worked stopped, cooking began. We'd have these wonderful meals together where we would eat the most delicious food. It was great! She would take a day or two off beforehand and she would cook these wonderful meals. We'd all go to the synagogue together, all be dressed 'to the nines'. For me, that was the time I had my mom home, and I had my parents... it was wonderful. I had a great life. I *have* a great life."

Karen recalled a photograph of her and her mother dressed for a special outing to"Petticoat Lane."

"'Petticoat Lane' was a street downtown where Harshfeld's was, which was the Saks Fifth Avenue of its day in Kansas City. In the '50s when you went downtown," said Karen, "the women wore a hat and gloves and were dressed, you know, 'to the nines.' So there was a picture taken,.. .1 don't have a lot of pictures of myself as a child. I don't know that Sam has a lot of them either. This was a portrait, I can't be five, and I have a coat on and black paten shoes, white socks and I have a little purse. My mother has her coat on and her purse and heels and a hat. It was like... 'the ladies', this cute black and white photo. It's just adorable. And it was so special! Because she worked, it was so special."

Another special childhood memory Karen has of her mother is of Maria making a rare visit to a Brownie Troop meeting. "Other mothers were constantly at school. You know, for PTA, or for serving lunch or that kind of thing. My mother never-could. So one time after school, I was in Brownies and they were teaching us to sew, a merit badge for sewing. So I asked my mom, and she came home from work early and came to the Brownie troop. Then she taught all the girls to sew. She didn't look like June Cleaver. She was in business attire, high heels and her hair done, and I was so, so, so proud.

"I think the largest influence on me, of my mother as a career woman, was that if I could swing it at all, I would stay home with my children. Exactly the opposite. And fortunately, I was able to stay home with my children. Many women, as I was raising my children, chose to begin a career or to continue whatever career they had before, and I said, 'Enjoy yourself,' because I was going to be a career mother."

"Our parents gave us great values. 'Family first. Education second.' All wrapped around your faith. You knew the rules and you knew the consequences of breaking the rules. We were not the 'iffy' generation, (laughs).

"What was memorable and a constant from my earliest childhood to today was that we were a very faith-based family. And our celebrations, our rituals, our coming together, were all around our religion. For example, we have one holiday called 'Purim'. Other people would call it like a Halloween. It was a dress up holiday, a costume holiday as a remembrance of something that happened in our history.

"So, you know my mother, who worked six days a week, but for that holiday, she came home early. I remember how she sewed. My brother and I had costumes. No one in Hollywood had such costumes the way we had costumes. I was Queen Esther. I had a gold taffeta dress. A full dress with ruffles, a red satin cape with gold brocade, gold ric-rac kind of all around the frame of it, with buttons or jewels sewed all around the front. I had a crown. I had long hair that I normally wore in braids, but for this holiday, she sat me on a chair and she took a curling iron. It was the kind you put on the stove to heat. And she would sit for - I don't know how long it would take - but because a Queen had those curls, I had a head full of these long curls.

"And my brother, who was a king, had a crown and she had taken out white stuff, like cotton or whatever, and made a big beard. He had a white garment, like a pant but with a long garment, then a big belt. He was this king person."

Maria chimes in with, "You know history,.. .King Ahasuerus!"

"The point of the story," said Karen, "is that there are serious holidays and there are fun holidays, but we all came together with family and food. Sometimes relatives would come from other cities for a holiday. It's such a warm memory and and it carries us through to today, because now the same things that my mom did for all of us, now I do. It's kind of all moved to my house. She passed the mantle of the holidays.

"At family functions that there was always music and dancing. And my father would take me to dance. My father was a fabulous dancer. Fred Astaire kind of dancer. He loved dancing. I love music and I love dancing but I'm just terrible at it. And so, when I would dance with my father, he told me I had two left feet. So maybe I wasn't as coordinated as everybody else.

"One thing about my parents, was how my father adored my mother. My father adored my mother just like out of a movie. He just adored her.

"My father was always very generous in a quiet way. He came from a wealthy business family in Europe before the war. But when he came to this country, after the war, no one had anything. For a number of years, it was pretty hard times. So when he became the employer, versus, the employee, he was a very, very generous person. When it came to holidays or something like that, there'd be a few people that worked for him that, you know, weren't doing so well. And when he passed away, people came out of the woodwork to say, 'you don't know how your father slipped us some money,' or 'brought us a turkey that we wouldn't have had for our family,' or 'gave me his top coat.'

"He'd just take things over like on Christmas or Thanksgiving. Maybe sacks of food and clothes for this fella. You know, things he had had from the year before, like a suit, or coat or whatever. I don't think any of us knew about that, at least I didn't know about that for years. He did it in a more quiet way.

"Now my mother was one of those people that, when she walked in the room, she just kind of sucked in all the light. My mother did philanthropy and she did all the decorating at the Synagogue for the dinners and that type of thing. They called her the 'flower lady.' And she was always on committees there; fundraising committees."

Karen was a 12-year-old when Ida Pearle Devinki arrived on August 5, 1963.

"I was definitely the surprise of 1963," said Ida. "I was a 'late in life' baby. I know that I was not planned or expected. The story went that nobody knew Maria was pregnant until she was like 5 months pregnant. I don't know if it was because she was keeping it a secret or she really didn't know. She was 43 when I was born. I think my father was 50. Karen was 12. Sam was 17."

Sam recalls finding out from his grandmother, who, in a great state of agitation, rhetorically asked, "Do you know what your father did to your mother!?!"

Ida would only spend about a year and a half in the house at 1008 w. 70th Terrace. In 1964 (the anniversary DVD says it was 1965) their father, Fred, suffered a heart attack. Unable to climb stairs as a result, the family moved from their two story home to a 3-bedroom ranch at the corner of 67th and State Line.

Recalling the heart attack, Sam was awed by his father's strength.

"He drove himself to the hospital. I mean, he knew something was wrong, but he didn't know what. He had had a heart attack. He drove himself to the hospital and he called my mother and we all went rushing up there. I remember walking into the hospital room and here is his doctor, Harry Wahl, smoking a cigarette. And here's my father, lying in bed, smoking a cigarette! On the same day he had his heart attack! In those days, believe it or not, even in the mid-'60s, what they did to treat a heart attack was bed rest. That was it. I mean, they didn't do anything with your arteries or anything like that. There was no open heart surgery."

From his hospital bed, Fred urged Maria to go ahead with pending contracts on the Thomas Carlile, the James Russell Lowell building and 700 Ward Parkway on the Plaza -that property became Devinki Real Estate headquarters until the move to Plaza Point in 1981.

"What we didn't know then was that the heart attack had damaged the lower chamber of his heart. He literally lived on 2/3rd of a heart for the last 28 years of his life. This guy was so strong that he could function on 2/3rds of a heart. It caused his heart to enlarge and congestive heart failure eventually killed him at the age of 79. But from age 51 to 79, he survived with 2/3rds of a heart!"

Ida would also attest to the strength of Fred Devinki, long after his heart attack.

"When I say he was strong, I'm not exaggerating," said Ida. "The man was physically very, very strong. I mean, he was not huge in stature or anything like that. He wasn't like 'working out' kind of strong. He was just physically a strong man.

"I remember, we used to wear overalls; 'painter pants' overalls, the white ones, you know? I mean, they were popular, right? My father tore a pair of those in half in front of me. He said, 'You're not a painter. I can afford to buy you clothes.' At the time it was a little frightening."

Her father's outburst had less to do with making a fashion statement than remembering his own time as a painter. Perhaps his last day as a painter. And Fred did not want his daughter dressed like that no matter how popular it might be with the world at large. Make no mistake, appearances were always important to keep up in the Devinki household.

"My mother always had me dressed for pre-school. And I mean dressed," Ida recalled. "I had black paten leather shoes and tights and dresses and my hair was done. I was always 'to the nines.'"

Ida attended preschool at the synagogue, Kehilath Israel, and then to Border Starr elementary in the Kansas City, Missouri School District.

"I always had a hard time in school. I had difficulty educationally. And I remember Bobby Galanda said to me once - we started public school together at Border Starr and we used to car pool with them - it was years and years and years later, he said to me, 'Yeah, I remember when we were little,' he goes, 'you didn't speak English.' And it's not that I didn't speak English, I think that I had such a thick accent on my English because that's what I was hearing...from my mother, my father. They both had thick accents. And the language in the house most of the time wasn't English, it was Yiddish. So, as a child, not that I didn't speak English or I didn't understand English, but I think my first language was a combination of the two.

"I went to Border Star. I didn't do well in public school. My parents tried to send me to the Hebrew Academy. The Hebrew Academy at the time wouldn't take me, because they said that my Hebrew skills were so poor that there was no way they could catch me up to the grade I would need to be.

"Then they tried to send me to Sunset Hill. Not quite sure why I didn't end up there. I didn't want to go there. The girls' side was Sunset Hill and the boys' side was Pem Day."

Ida ended up going to school at Loretto, where her friend Jamie "Doogee" Daugherty attended. The Daugherty's had lived next door on 70th Terrace, said Ida, "that's how we found out about Loretto."

Loretto was an Irish Catholic girls' school, run by the Nuns of Loretto, but it was not run as a stereotypical parochial school. At the time, it was new. "Somebody would have called it 'new fangled education'," said Ida. "You didn't really have classes or grades. They had pods. You had 1st through 3 in one pod and then 4th through 5th in another pod. It was group learning. They were nuns. The majority of them were very upbeat nuns. They didn't wear the habits. Only the old, old nuns wore the habits. And it was very '70s, modern, you know? Like, we had streakers!

"It was considered alternative education, in a sense. I started there in 3rd grade. And the reason my parents sent me there was because they thought that they (the nuns) would work with me more. And I gotta be honest, in one respect they were right. I had two nuns, Sister Mary and Sister Susan, who would study with me and work with me relentlessly. I think my parents were always afraid I'd come home with a big cross on me; 'the nice little Jewish girl in the Irish Catholic girls school.' But at the time, they (the nuns) were really respectful of me. And really, there wasn't a lot of 'religion' in this school. It was just religiously run. They would have a mass of some sort once in a blue moon, but it would be because mere was an earthquake somewhere, or some horrific tragedy somewhere. So they'd bring the whole lower school together to pray that things should be good for these people, whatever horrific thing had happened to them.

"Everything always seemed to be done on a group, or a global level.

Loretto used to be all girls. Then they started letting in boys. I went there for 5 years, through middle school, or junior high, whatever they called it men. At the time, we still lived on the Missouri side. Sam lived in Mission Hills, on the Kansas side. Now I don't know if it's fact or fiction, but what I was told - because of the way the law was written, how old my father was, this, that and the other - that somehow they made Sam my legal guardian. And in making Sam my legal guardian, I started to go to school in Shawnee Mission. I went to 8th and 9th grade at Indian Hills. Then I went to Shawnee Mission East High School.

"The house that we lived in on 67th and State Line was an awesome, awesome house. It was so 'James Bond' I can't even tell you. It was so cool! It was '60s modern, a ranch style house. The whole back yard was California slate stone, and the front part was California stone and it had wood floors and the living room was wood paneling. It was called 'zebra wood.' It went in a 'v.' It was panels, but the coloring went in a 'v.' It was gorgeous. Absolutely gorgeous. I mean, if I could rebuild this house, in a New York minute, I would rebuild this house.

"What was so 'James Bond' about it was the TV mounted in the wall. On each side of the TV were fish tanks in the wall. And above the fish tanks were speakers, stereo speakers. They were like doors over the fish tanks, but you couldn't see them really, you just saw the grates. And all of this was wired through the back wall. The back wall was the hallway to the bedrooms where there were closets. And all these wires were in the closets.

"So all of this is in the wall, and underneath were these two huge doors that opened up. Inside the doors were shelves. And in the center, was a stainless steel sliding sink. You pulled a lever and the sink slid forward and the shelves had liquor. It was a bar! It was so 'James Bond'! I mean, all you needed was the electric remote control switch! It was major cool.

"Anyway, we lived in that house on 67th, Sam lived in Mission Hills, and then something happened with either the law or how old I was, I'm not sure, but we had to move to Kansas if I was going to stay in Kansas' schools. So that's when my parents bought the house that my mother lives in now, 8415 Ensley Place; 83rd & Mission. They bought a two story, 5-bedroom house for the three of us. It was a story and a half. It had two bedrooms downstairs and three bedrooms upstairs. The master bedroom was downstairs. The whole first floor is like a two bedroom ranch. We moved there when I was 15, when I started going to Shawnee Mission East.

During the 1970s, Devinki Real Estate would purchase four other Plaza properties. Before the deeds were even closed, Fred and Maria had sold two of them. And used the profits to pay for the other two.

While going to law school at UMKC in the early '70s, Sam was manager of the 400 unit Barcelona West apartment complex. After graduating law school at the University of Oklahoma, Sam put even more of his energies into the family business.

In the 1980s, Sam negotiated a very good deal on the "Riviera," now known as the "Hemmingway" on Ward Parkway. By 1985, Devinki Real Estate was the second largest apartment owner on the Plaza. While apartment management had proven to be a good business, at age 65, Maria was looking for the next big thing. She decided it was land. Her first major holding was 80 acres of Johnson County farm land. At the same time, at Sam's urging, the company expanded into commercial real estate with the purchase of Twin Trails Shopping Center in Olathe. In Maria's "Golden Years", they added a Kmart in North Kansas City, plus a 250,000 sq.ft. warehouse in Joplin, Missouri and a WalMart center in Manhattan, Kansas, along with three more apartment complexes in Raytown; Coach Lamp Corner, Raytown Village and Somerset Village.

"My parents were always working, always working," said Ida. "We joke about it, but it's really the truth, I was raised by the cleaning lady. My mother will tell you that at 9-months-old I was potty trained. And she swears by it. She swears! I was like, 'how the hell could that be?' And it's because of the cleaning lady, I guarantee you.

"Back then, cleaning ladies were different. Today, a cleaning lady comes and cleans your house. *This* was a 'housekeeper.' Someone who came in and not only cleaned your house, she babysat, she prepared food. She came and stayed 'til 5:00 o'clock, Monday through Friday.

And when Ida outgrew her housekeepers, she became a trend setter.

"I was the latchkey kid. The bus would drop me off and I'd be home alone. When you're left alone a bit growing up, a lot of ways you become self-sufficient. A lot of ways you can get yourself in trouble. I didn't get into a whole lot of trouble. I was pretty much your good kid.

"I did have one 'stay-out-past-midnight' episode and really, that was because I'd never been given a formal curfew. They never said you had to be home by 'X'. And I remember I came home, Sam's car was in the driveway and I looked at my date and said, 'One of two things are going on. Either I'm in trouble or somebody's dead.' And I'll never forget, he says, 'This is okay. I'll fix it. I'll take care of it.'

"He walked me up to the door -1 was 15 - he didn't even have a chance to open the door... and my mother was there. She's in her pink robe, toilet paper wrapped around her hair, with her pink hairnet. And he very politely says, 'I had trouble with my car. I apologize for bringing Ida home so late. Good night.'

"He leaves, I walk in, and am just waiting to be massacred, just waiting. My father walks around the corner. He looks at me and says, 'Once. Just once. And never again.' And he walks back to his bedroom.

"My mother had a few words. Sam 'ripped me a new one,' and then everybody went to

bed. It was a Friday night. In the morning, Sam would pick up my mother and me for

services, because my father would go early. I remember him asking me, 'What did daddy

do to you?'

"And I go, 'Nothing.'

"He said, 'What do you mean?'

"I said, 'You were there. You heard what he said! That's all he said! That's all he did!'

"And Sam goes, 'You're just...! You got lucky!!!

"I got the fear of G-d in me. I was never late again. Ever.

"It's funny, they did complement each other very well, (Fred & Maria). They really did. And I know that he loved her. He would do anything for her.

"We'd be making a meal and, for one reason or another, my mother couldn't make a grocery list if her life depended on it. She thinks about what she's making; the 5-10 items that she needs for that, and that's as far as it goes. She would send him to the grocery store 3 or 4 times to go get what she needed to make what she was making. Whatever she said, he would do it. - Not necessarily that he wouldn't complain about it, but he'd do it."

While Ida knew how her parents dealt with the present and the future, there was a lot about their past that she didn't know.

"I don't think, as a child, I ever realized that my parents were Holocaust survivors. I didn't know what that meant. Didn't really have a clue until I was a young adult. They didn't talk about it. I mean, I knew my parents were from Europe. In Sunday School, they start teaching you certain things about it. But I mean, I had to have been 9 or 10 before they start talking about it in school, and then, it probably wasn't until I was at least 12 or 13 before I made the connection."

One thing that might have tipped her off, is the support her parents gave to the State of Israel Bond program promoting economic independence for the State of Israel. On November 11th, 1979, Fred and Maria were awarded a plaque with the Shield of Jehuda to honor their gifts and commitment.

CPSIA information can be obtained
at www.ICGtesting.com
Printed in the USA
BVHW041457260922
647995BV00003B/304